THE *Washington DC* HANDBOOK

National Park Service
U.S. Department of the Interior

THE *Washington DC* HANDBOOK

Eastern National provides quality educational products and services to the visitors to America's national parks and other public trusts.

Visit us at www.eParks.com.

The Donning Company Publishers
184 Business Park Drive, Suite 206
Virginia Beach, VA 23462

Library of Congress Cataloging-in-Publication Data

The Washington, DC handbook.
p. cm.
"Pamela Koch, editor"—T.p. verso.
Includes index.
ISBN-13: 978-1-57864-396-7 (soft cover : alk. paper)
ISBN-10: 1-57864-396-1 (soft cover : alk. paper)
1. National parks and reserves—Washington Region—Guidebooks. 2. Historic sites—Washington Region—Guidebooks. 3. National monuments—Washington (D.C.)—Guidebooks. 4. Washington Region—Guidebooks. 5. Washington (D.C.)—Guidebooks. 6. Washington Region—History, Local. I. Koch, Pamela. II. Donning Company Publishers.
F203.5.A1W325 2009
917.5304'42—dc22

2006031794

Printed in the United States of America at Walsworth Publishing Company

TABLE OF CONTENTS

WELCOME TO THE GREATER WASHINGTON NATIONAL PARKS

Welcome to one of the greatest cities and regions in the world.

With this handbook, you are well prepared to enjoy the wonderful variety of experiences that Washington, D.C., has to offer. We hope that your visit will be both memorable and enjoyable and that this handbook will enable you to make the most of your time with us.

The Greater Washington National Parks are comprised of hundreds of National Park Service sites in the District of Columbia, Virginia, West Virginia, Maryland, and Pennsylvania. These parks are special places and contain wonderful natural retreats, icons of our democracy, wonderfully preserved Civil War battlefields, historic sites, and world-class venues for the performing arts. As you can see, there is something for everyone in the Greater Washington National Parks, and it is our privilege to be the stewards of these significant public treasures. These are your parks, your trails, your memorials, and your parkways—enjoy them often and thank you for your support in the preservation of our collective heritage.

National Park Service Employees
National Capital Region

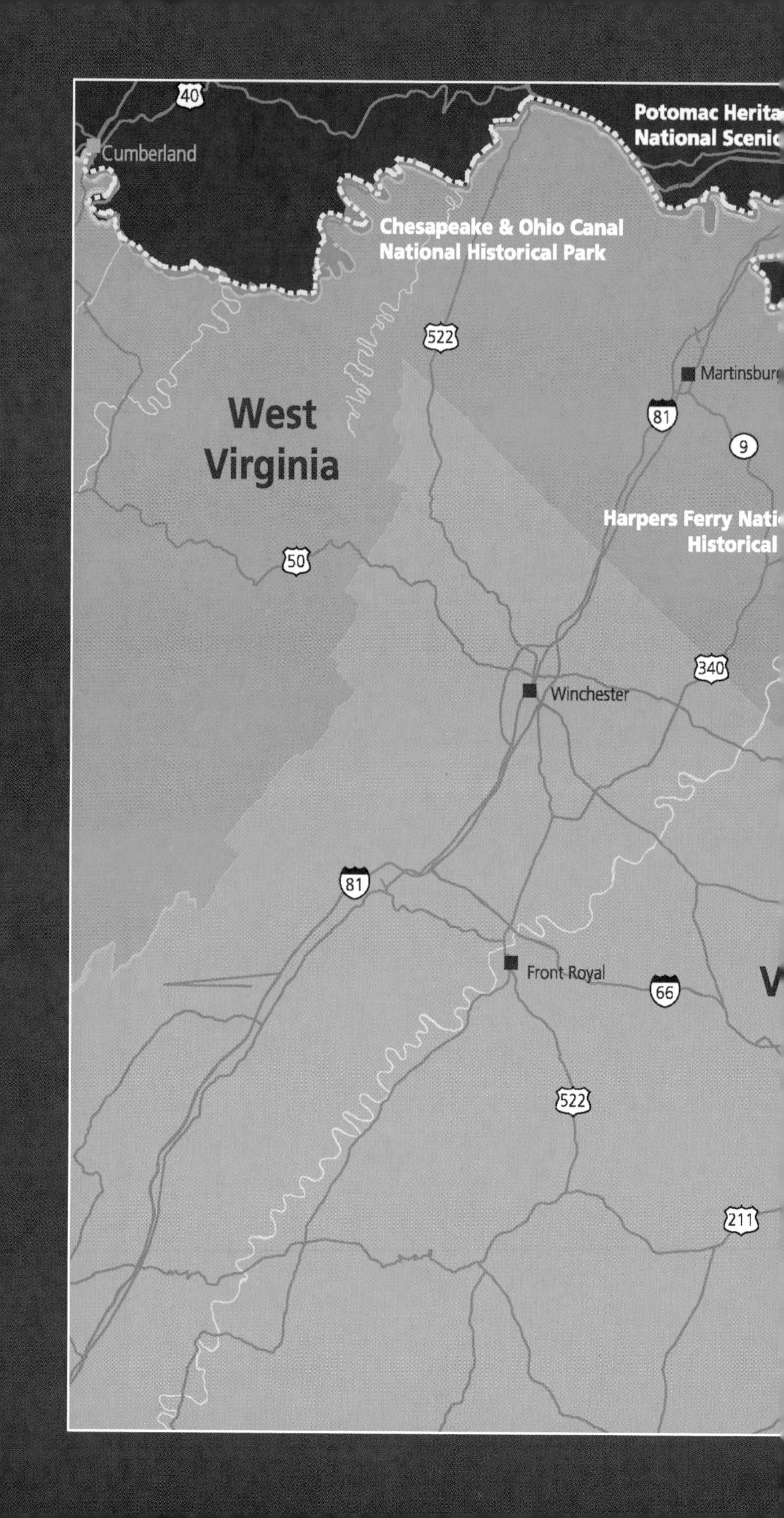
40
Cumberland
Potomac Herita
National Scenic
Chesapeake & Ohio Canal
National Historical Park
522
Martinsburg
81
9
West
Virginia
Harpers Ferry Nati
Historical
50
340
Winchester
81
Front Royal
66
V
522
211

Regional Map
Catoctin
untain Park
rstown
15
140
Westminster
40
ietam National
lefield
Frederick
Maryland
70
340
Monocacy National
Battlefield
695
270
15
95
Chesapeake & Ohio Canal
National Historical Park
Baltimore-Washington
Parkway
Leesburg
Rockville
7
George Washington
Memorial Parkway
Rock Creek
Park
Greenbelt
Park
Wolf Trap National Park
for the Performing Arts
495
President's Park
National Mall &
Memorial Parks
National Capital
Parks - East
15
DC
Fairfax
Alexandria
95
s National
efield Park
Manassas
301
234
1
Fort
Washington Park
Piscataway
Park
Prince William
Forest Park
95
North
La Plata

Washington, in all its splendor and variety, welcomes you whether you are here for a day, a week, or longer. The city's attractions are so numerous that you will be challenged by the choices you have to make. Nearly every first-time visitor wants to tour the National Mall with its well-known museums and landmarks.

At these places, you will find a familiar face and friendly hand for most of the monuments, memorials, and parks in the Nation's Capital are managed by the very same National Park Service identified with the country's other natural, historical, and recreational treasures: Yellowstone, Grand Canyon, and nearly 400 other sites. In fact, many of Washington's parks are among the nation's oldest, for they date from the District of Columbia's establishment in 1790.

THE *Monumental* HEART OF THE CITY

With the inspiring World War II Memorial framing the scene, the Reflecting Pool points the way toward the impressive Lincoln Memorial.

In addition to the memorials and monuments, the National Park Service manages many lesser-known sites here, ranging from The Old Stone House in Georgetown to Kenilworth Park and Aquatic Gardens on the banks of the Anacostia River. Wherever you travel, you will meet the men and women of the National Park Service, so do not hesitate to ask these park rangers, maintenance workers, and mounted park police officers for assistance. They will do all they can to answer your questions and to help you make the most of your visit. The following guide, packed with details about the Washington area's national parks, is offered with that same friendly spirit.

www.nps.gov/nama

Jefferson Memorial

George Mason

Constitution Gardens

Old Post Office

Ericsson Statue

Three Servicemen Statue at the Vietnam Veterans Memorial

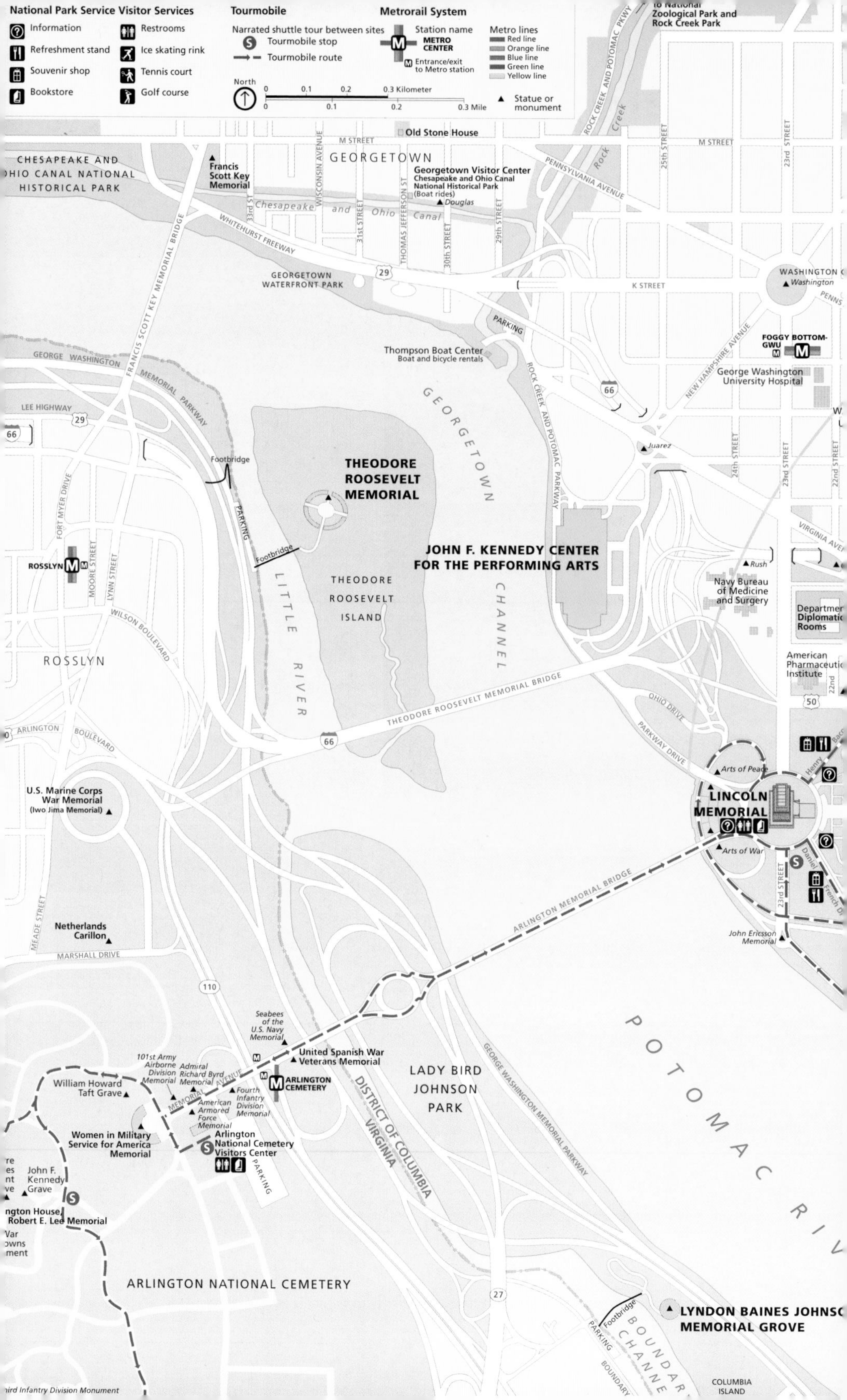
National Park Service Visitor Services
Information
Refreshment stand
Souvenir shop
Bookstore
Restrooms
Ice skating rink
Tennis court
Golf course
Tourmobile
Narrated shuttle tour between sites
Tourmobile stop
Tourmobile route
Metrorail System
Station name
METRO CENTER
Entrance/exit to Metro station
Metro lines
Red line
Orange line
Blue line
Green line
Yellow line
Statue or monument
North
0 0.1 0.2 0.3 Kilometer
0 0.1 0.2 0.3 Mile
Zoological Park and Rock Creek Park
Old Stone House
M STREET
GEORGETOWN
CHESAPEAKE AND OHIO CANAL NATIONAL HISTORICAL PARK
Francis Scott Key Memorial
Georgetown Visitor Center
Chesapeake and Ohio Canal National Historical Park
(Boat rides)
Douglas
Chesapeake and Ohio Canal
WHITEHURST FREEWAY
PENNSYLVANIA AVENUE
ROCK CREEK AND POTOMAC PKWY
Rock Creek
WISCONSIN AVENUE
33rd ST
31st STREET
THOMAS JEFFERSON ST
30th STREET
29th STREET
25th STREET
23rd STREET
GEORGETOWN WATERFRONT PARK
K STREET
WASHINGTON CIRCLE
Washington
PARKING
Thompson Boat Center
Boat and bicycle rentals
FOGGY BOTTOM-GWU
NEW HAMPSHIRE AVENUE
George Washington University Hospital
FRANCIS SCOTT KEY MEMORIAL BRIDGE
GEORGE WASHINGTON MEMORIAL PARKWAY
LEE HIGHWAY
GEORGETOWN CHANNEL
Footbridge
THEODORE ROOSEVELT MEMORIAL
ROCK CREEK AND POTOMAC PARKWAY
Juarez
24th STREET
22nd STREET
FORT MYER DRIVE
ROSSLYN
MOORE STREET
LYNN STREET
WILSON BOULEVARD
LITTLE RIVER
THEODORE ROOSEVELT ISLAND
JOHN F. KENNEDY CENTER FOR THE PERFORMING ARTS
VIRGINIA AVENUE
Rush
Navy Bureau of Medicine and Surgery
Department Diplomatic Rooms
American Pharmaceutical Institute
THEODORE ROOSEVELT MEMORIAL BRIDGE
OHIO DRIVE
PARKWAY DRIVE
ARLINGTON BOULEVARD
Arts of Peace
LINCOLN MEMORIAL
Arts of War
U.S. Marine Corps War Memorial (Iwo Jima Memorial)
ARLINGTON MEMORIAL BRIDGE
John Ericsson Memorial
MEADE STREET
Netherlands Carillon
MARSHALL DRIVE
Seabees of the U.S. Navy Memorial
United Spanish War Veterans Memorial
ARLINGTON CEMETERY
101st Army Airborne Division Memorial
Admiral Richard Byrd Memorial
MEMORIAL AVENUE
Fourth Infantry Division Memorial
American Armored Force Memorial
William Howard Taft Grave
Women in Military Service for America Memorial
Arlington National Cemetery Visitors Center
John F. Kennedy Grave
Robert E. Lee Memorial
LADY BIRD JOHNSON PARK
DISTRICT OF COLUMBIA
VIRGINIA
GEORGE WASHINGTON MEMORIAL PARKWAY
POTOMAC RIV
ARLINGTON NATIONAL CEMETERY
LYNDON BAINES JOHNSON MEMORIAL GROVE
BOUNDARY CHANNEL
COLUMBIA ISLAND
ird Infantry Division Monument

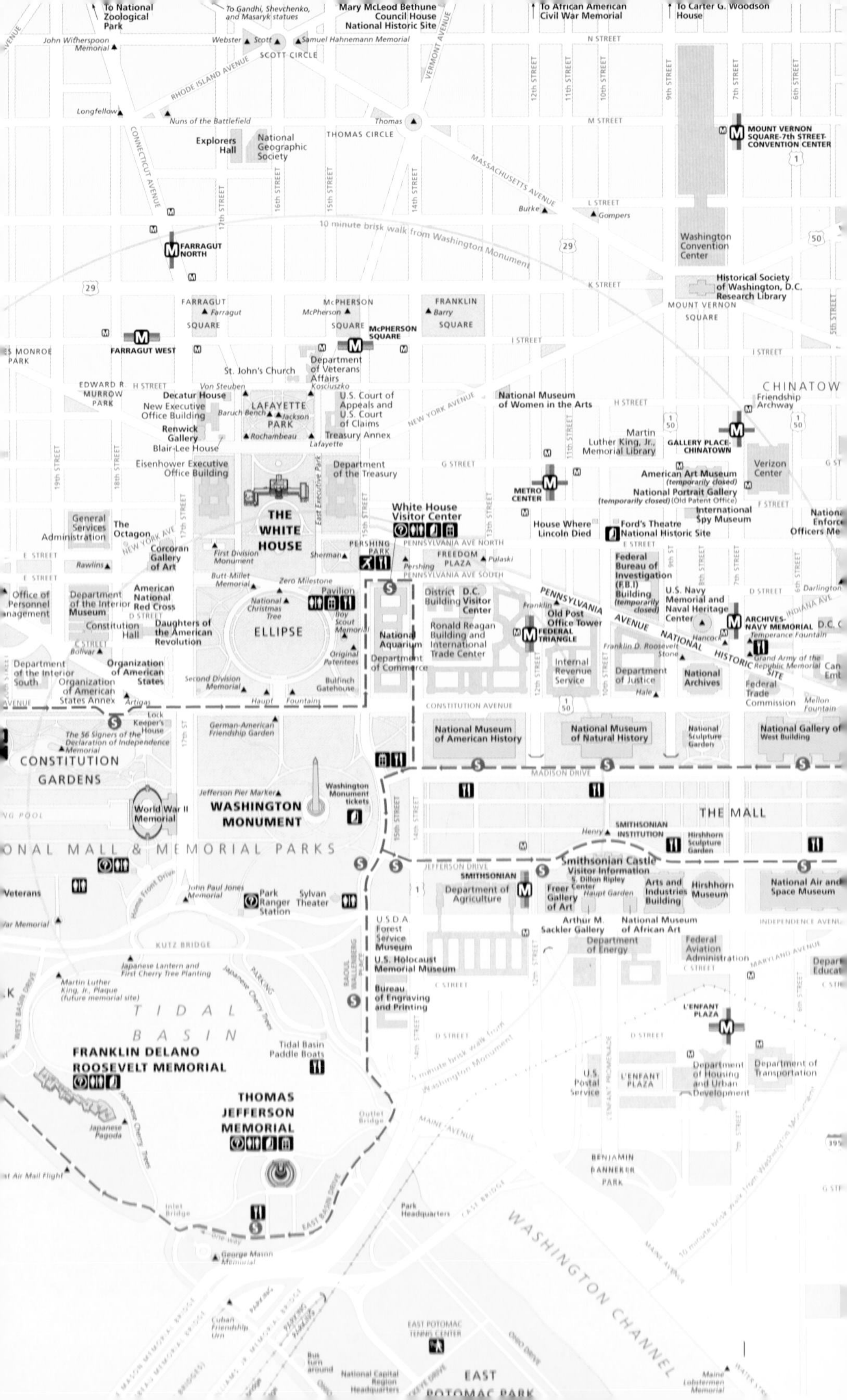
To National Zoological Park
To Gandhi, Shevchenko, and Masaryk statues
Mary McLeod Bethune Council House National Historic Site
To African American Civil War Memorial
To Carter G. Woodson House
John Witherspoon Memorial
Webster
Scott
Samuel Hahnemann Memorial
SCOTT CIRCLE
N STREET
RHODE ISLAND AVENUE
VERMONT AVENUE
Longfellow
Nuns of the Battlefield
Thomas
M STREET
Explorers Hall
National Geographic Society
THOMAS CIRCLE
CONNECTICUT AVENUE
MOUNT VERNON SQUARE-7th STREET-CONVENTION CENTER
MASSACHUSETTS AVENUE
17th STREET
16th STREET
15th STREET
14th STREET
13th STREET
12th STREET
11th STREET
10th STREET
9th STREET
7th STREET
6th STREET
5th STREET
L STREET
Burke
Gompers
10 minute brisk walk from Washington Monument
FARRAGUT NORTH
Washington Convention Center
K STREET
Historical Society of Washington, D.C. Research Library
MOUNT VERNON SQUARE
FARRAGUT SQUARE
Farragut
McPHERSON SQUARE
McPherson
McPHERSON SQUARE
FRANKLIN SQUARE
Barry
FARRAGUT WEST
I STREET
MONROE PARK
St. John's Church
Department of Veterans Affairs
CHINATOWN
Friendship Archway
EDWARD R. MURROW PARK
H STREET
Von Steuben
Decatur House
Kosciuszko
U.S. Court of Appeals and U.S. Court of Claims
NEW YORK AVENUE
National Museum of Women in the Arts
New Executive Office Building
LAFAYETTE PARK
Baruch Bench
Jackson
Renwick Gallery
Rochambeau
Lafayette
Treasury Annex
Martin Luther King, Jr., Memorial Library
GALLERY PLACE-CHINATOWN
Blair-Lee House
19th STREET
18th STREET
Eisenhower Executive Office Building
Department of the Treasury
G STREET
American Art Museum (temporarily closed)
Verizon Center
National Portrait Gallery (temporarily closed) (Old Patent Office)
METRO CENTER
F STREET
General Services Administration
The Octagon
THE WHITE HOUSE
East Executive Park
White House Visitor Center
International Spy Museum
House Where Lincoln Died
Ford's Theatre National Historic Site
National Law Enforcement Officers Memorial
E STREET
Corcoran Gallery of Art
First Division Monument
Sherman
PERSHING PARK
PENNSYLVANIA AVE NORTH
FREEDOM PLAZA
Pulaski
Pershing
PENNSYLVANIA AVE SOUTH
Rawlins
Butt-Millet Memorial
Zero Milestone
Federal Bureau of Investigation (F.B.I.) Building (temporarily closed)
Office of Personnel Management
Department of the Interior Museum
American National Red Cross
National Christmas Tree
Pavilion
District Building
D.C. Visitor Center
Franklin
PENNSYLVANIA AVENUE
Old Post Office Tower
U.S. Navy Memorial and Naval Heritage Center
D STREET
Darlington
INDIANA AVE
ARCHIVES-NAVY MEMORIAL
Temperance Fountain
Constitution Hall
Daughters of the American Revolution
ELLIPSE
Boy Scout Memorial
National Aquarium
Ronald Reagan Building and International Trade Center
FEDERAL TRIANGLE
Franklin D. Roosevelt Stone
NATIONAL HISTORIC SITE
Hancock
Grand Army of the Republic Memorial
C STREET
Bolivar
Original Patentees
Department of Commerce
Department of the Interior South
Organization of American States
Internal Revenue Service
Department of Justice
National Archives
Federal Trade Commission
Organization of American States Annex
Second Division Memorial
Bulfinch Gatehouse
Hale
Mellon Fountain
Artigas
Haupt
Fountains
CONSTITUTION AVENUE
Lock Keeper's House
German-American Friendship Garden
National Museum of American History
National Museum of Natural History
National Sculpture Garden
National Gallery of Art West Building
The 56 Signers of the Declaration of Independence Memorial
CONSTITUTION GARDENS
MADISON DRIVE
World War II Memorial
Jefferson Pier Marker
WASHINGTON MONUMENT
Washington Monument tickets
THE MALL
SMITHSONIAN INSTITUTION
Henry
Hirshhorn Sculpture Garden
NATIONAL MALL & MEMORIAL PARKS
Smithsonian Castle Visitor Information Center
JEFFERSON DRIVE
SMITHSONIAN
S. Dillon Ripley Center
Veterans
John Paul Jones Memorial
Park Ranger Station
Sylvan Theater
Department of Agriculture
Freer Gallery of Art
Haupt Garden
Arts and Industries Building
Hirshhorn Museum
National Air and Space Museum
Home Front Drive
INDEPENDENCE AVENUE
USDA Forest Service Museum
Arthur M. Sackler Gallery
National Museum of African Art
KUTZ BRIDGE
Department of Energy
U.S. Holocaust Memorial Museum
Federal Aviation Administration
Japanese Lantern and First Cherry Tree Planting
MARYLAND AVENUE
Martin Luther King, Jr., Plaque (future memorial site)
RAOUL WALLENBERG PLACE
Bureau of Engraving and Printing
L'ENFANT PLAZA
TIDAL BASIN
WEST BASIN DRIVE
Tidal Basin Paddle Boats
FRANKLIN DELANO ROOSEVELT MEMORIAL
Department of Transportation
Department of Housing and Urban Development
U.S. Postal Service
L'ENFANT PLAZA
L'ENFANT PROMENADE
5 minute brisk walk from Washington Monument
THOMAS JEFFERSON MEMORIAL
Outlet Bridge
MAINE AVENUE
Japanese Pagoda
Japanese Cherry Trees
BENJAMIN BANNEKER PARK
Air Mail Flight
Inlet Bridge
Park Headquarters
EAST BASIN DRIVE
WASHINGTON CHANNEL
George Mason Memorial
10 minute brisk walk from Washington Monument
Cuban Friendship Urn
EAST POTOMAC TENNIS CENTER
Bus turn around
National Capital Region Headquarters
EAST POTOMAC PARK
Maine Lobstermen Memorial

NATIONAL MALL & MEMORIAL PARKS

Washington, D.C.

National Mall & Memorial Parks contains some of the oldest protected parkland in the National Park Service. The areas within National Mall & Memorial Parks provide visitors with many opportunities to commemorate presidential legacies, honor the courage and sacrifice of war veterans, and celebrate the United States' commitment to freedom and equality.

National Mall & Memorial Parks is responsible for more than 1,000 acres of some of the United States' highly significant natural and cultural resources. The sites of National Mall & Memorial Parks are cherished symbols of our nation, known worldwide and depicted on everything from currency to the nightly news. Located in the core of the Nation's Capital, National Mall & Memorial Parks administers, interprets, maintains, and preserves the Washington Monument; the Lincoln, Thomas Jefferson, and Franklin Delano Roosevelt memorials; the Ulysses S. Grant Memorial; the World War II Memorial; the Korean War Veterans Memorial; the Vietnam Veterans Memorial; Pennsylvania Avenue from the Capitol to the White House; the National Mall; East and West Potomac Parks; Constitution Gardens; 60 statues; and numerous other historic sites, memorials, and parklands.

National Mall & Memorial Parks is responsible for significant maintenance and preservation support for the White House as well as the U.S. Navy Memorial. National Mall & Memorial Parks' origins are as old as the capital city itself. The open space and parklands envisioned by Pierre L'Enfant's plan, which George Washington commissioned, created an ideal stage for national expressions of remembrance, observance, and demonstrations of freedom. With everything from colossal monuments to commemorative gardens, and from presidential inaugurals to civil rights protests, National

Mall & Memorial Parks hosts history in the making. Numerous First Amendment activities and special events are held in the park each year. The park continually evolves as Americans seek new ways to recognize their heritage.

National Mall & Memorial Parks contains more than 80 historic structures and more than 150 major named historic parks, squares, circles, and triangles. Park resources include the 2,000 American elms that line the National Mall and the 3,000 internationally renowned Japanese cherry trees that grace the Tidal Basin. Gardens that are botanical showplaces display thousands of tulips, pansies, and annuals in over 170 flowerbeds. Thirty-five ornamental pools and fountains range from the simple to the sublime. This impressive mingling of natural and cultural resources has made our Nation's Capital one of the more heavily visited and photographed places in the world.

National Mall & Memorial Parks offers Americans the opportunity to get in touch with their heritage. Thousands of visitors including schoolchildren, families, foreign visitors, veterans, and recreational users come to the park daily. They take advantage of interpretive programming presented by park rangers, park exhibits, publications, orientation services, and panoramic views from the Washington Monument and the Old Post Office Tower. White House, State Department, and congressional staffs use these same services to give foreign dignitaries exposure to American history and culture. National Mall & Memorial Parks is responsible for 43 ball fields where local clubs play softball, soccer, rugby, field hockey, volleyball, and polo. Residents and visitors enthusiastically pursue other recreational opportunities throughout the park, including jogging, biking, picnicking, golf, swimming, tennis, paddle boating, ice skating, and fishing.

WASHINGTON MONUMENT

Washington, D.C.

Proposals for honoring George Washington were made with growing regularity after his death in 1799. Pierre L'Enfant had included plans for an equestrian statue of Washington at the intersection of the Capitol's east-west axis and the White House's north-south axis as part of his design, but Washington had rejected it. The idea surfaced in 1816, 1819, 1824, 1825, and 1832, the centennial of his birth. The collapse of the 1832 proposal led George Watterston, the Librarian of Congress, to found the Washington National Monument Society to raise money and construct the memorial. Robert Mills won the design competition. His plan called for a shaft 600 feet high, surrounded at its base by a circular building that was to serve as a national pantheon containing statues of notable figures in American history. Atop the door, Mills planned to install a huge figure of Washington driving a chariot. Meanwhile, the fund-raising lagged, and Congress balked at providing federal land. In 1848, these problems were resolved and ground was broken. Work had proceeded to the 150-foot level by 1854, when the "Know-Nothings," an anti-Catholic, anti-foreign political party, seized the monument because Pope Pius IX had sent a block of marble from Rome's Temple of Concord to be set into the interior wall with other memorial stones from foreign, state, and local governments and private organizations. The papal stone disappeared, and work on the monument also stopped. Work resumed in 1876 and proceeded at a good pace. The monument was dedicated February 21, 1885, with Robert Winthrop, who had spoken at the laying of the cornerstone 40 years earlier, giving the address. The monument was officially opened October 9, 1888.

As it stands today, the Washington Monument is a hollow obelisk, a four-sided pillar that tapers as it rises 500 feet to meet a pyramidion 55 feet 5 1/8 inches tall. The monument is the world's tallest freestanding stone structure. Most of the exterior stone is from Maryland. When work resumed on the obelisk in 1876, marble from the Maryland quarry could not be obtained; so matching marble was found in Massachusetts and laid for 13 courses. The Maryland marble again became available and was used to finish off the remainder of the monument. The new marble, however, has weathered to a slightly different shade, making it easy to see the two different stages of construction. The top of the monument is a 100-ounce cap of aluminum, the largest piece cast to that time.

www.nps.gov/wamo

The Washington Monument and its circle of 50 American flags symbolize the importance that George Washington placed on the American Union.

With the Washington Monument in the background, the columns, victory pavilions, and sculptural elements of the World War II Memorial testify to the unprecedented unity and sacrifice among the states and territories during the war.

WORLD WAR II MEMORIAL

Washington, D.C.

Almost 50 years after the war, legislation was passed that resulted in this testament to the sacrifices made by the American people during World War II. As troops returned home in the 1940s, communities across the nation honored their veterans by various means. Ultimately, local tributes were reinforced by federal efforts as it became much easier for Americans to visit their Nation's Capital. With new memorials honoring other wars, it became apparent that World War II deserved a prominent spot. On May 25, 1993, President Bill Clinton signed Public Law 103-32, which authorized the building of a memorial. Federal money was authorized to the amount of $16 million. However, the American Battle Monuments Commission initiated a grand fund-raising campaign. An additional $181 million was collected by generous donations from a grateful nation.

Despite serious wrangling over site placement, the area just east of the Reflecting Pool was chosen. Construction of architect Friedrich St.Florian's design began in September

2001, continuing until spring 2004. On May 29, 2004, President George W. Bush accepted the memorial on behalf of the nation. Thousands of veterans and their families made the pilgrimage to the dedication ceremony.

The ceremonial entrance along 17th Street holds an announcement marker. Looking west, two paths lie before the visitor. The southern is lined with bronze bas-reliefs depicting images of the war in the Pacific melded with home front images, while the north reflects the Atlantic theater and home front. Symbolic elements are overwhelming in the plaza. Quotations from leaders of the war adorn the memorial walls. The Rainbow Pool, present since the 1920s, was incorporated into the memorial's construction. It reinforces the war's scope, separating the Atlantic and Pacific pavilions that anchor the northern and southern sides of the memorial, respectively. In the pavilions, four eagles hold an ancient symbol of victory, a laurel wreath.

The field of over 4,000 gold stars at the west end is the centerpiece. Each star is a tribute to 100 Americans who made the ultimate sacrifice. The inscription reads, "Here we mark the price of freedom." Pillars representing the 48 states and eight territories in the United States during World War II surround the stars in honor guard formation. The first state that ratified the Constitution, Delaware, occupies a place of honor to the right of the stars as one faces the plaza. Pennsylvania, the second state to do so, is to the left. The remaining states and territories follow suit. Each pillar possesses two wreaths. One of wheat reinforces our agricultural output, while one of oak represents our strength in industry. The pillars stand alone, reflective of state individuality, yet an underlying rope ties them into an indivisible union. The nation enjoyed unprecedented unity during this time of crisis.

www.nps.gov/wwii

An engraved American eagle, inspired by the Great Seal of the United States, greets visitors to the World War II Memorial.

DISTRICT OF COLUMBIA WAR MEMORIAL

Washington, D.C.

The grounds of the District of Columbia War Memorial are always open. This modest memorial, half-hidden among the trees and bushes of West Potomac Park, honors the armed forces of the District of Columbia who served in World War I.

The war had ended on November 11, 1918, a date first remembered each year as Armistice Day, and now remembered as Veterans Day. Soon, city leaders began casting about for a way to honor the local men and women who had served. Eventually, the Commission of Fine Arts chose the site for a memorial, and architect Frederick H. Brooke was given the task of designing it.

Mr. Brooke planned a Greek temple, with a domed roof and 12 Doric columns. It was 47 feet high and 44 feet in diameter. The floor was made large enough to accommodate any military bands that might want to play there. Along the base were carved the names of the 487 Washingtonians who fell in battle, while a time capsule in the cornerstone preserved the names of all 26,048 who served.

On April 11, 1926, the city launched a massive fund-raising appeal for $200,000, to be raised solely through private donations. Money came in from private citizens, as well as civic groups and labor unions. Construction began on April 17, 1931. James Baird Company, the contractors, used white marble from Danby, Vermont.

President Herbert Hoover dedicated the memorial on November 11, 1931. John Philip Sousa conducted the U.S. Marine Band with no doubt rousing renditions of "Stars and Stripes Forever" and the "Star-Spangled Banner"—the official National Anthem in 1931.

Since then, the memorial has led a quiet, often overlooked existence. Bands have indeed played there every now and then, and occasionally, veterans groups still have ceremonies there.

www.nps.gov/nama

The classic simplicity of the memorial fittingly demonstrates the service and sacrifice of Washingtonians during the Great War.

JOHN PAUL JONES MEMORIAL

Washington, D.C.

A bold captain—fearless and brave even when facing the superior British Royal Navy—John Paul Jones achieved lasting fame during the American Revolution. The audacious Jones attacked the Scottish coast, defeated the HMS *Drake* in battle on the Irish Sea and, while commanding the *Bonhomme Richard*, captured the HMS *Serapis* during a spectacular engagement fought within view of the British shore. Celebrated throughout the United States, Jones provoked fear among the British. Perhaps Jones's greatest contribution to American independence was that he became a hero precisely when the cause needed one. On April 17, 1912, President William Howard Taft dedicated the John Paul Jones Memorial. It became the first memorial in the new Potomac Park. To this day, the U.S. Navy reveres Jones as a hero who exemplified bravery, daring, and devotion to duty despite overwhelming odds.

www.nps.gov/nama

Surrounded by strong nautical elements, the Jones statue accurately depicts the man standing defiantly upon the deck of a ship during battle.

LINCOLN MEMORIAL

Washington, D.C.

There never was any question that there should be a memorial to Lincoln, but where to put it and what it should be were questions that caused much debate. The present location at the west end of the National Mall balancing the Capitol on the east seems logical today, but at the turn of the 20th century, this was a marshy expanse of land.

In 1911, the Lincoln Memorial Commission chaired by President William Howard Taft began work on the memorial. For a site, the commission chose West Potomac Park, which had been drained and reclaimed from the Potomac River. Shortly afterwards, the commission decided upon Henry Bacon as the architect, and the cornerstone was laid February 12, 1915. As work on the foundation proceeded, the commissioners searched for a sculptor and eventually agreed upon Daniel Chester French. French wrestled with the problem of how to present the figure of Lincoln. Should it be a standing figure, and if so, what pose would be best? Or would a seated figure be more appropriate to the structure? Finally, French settled on a seated figure brooding over the burdens of the Civil War. The original specifications called

for a 10-foot high figure, but French soon realized that a statue that size would be dwarfed in Bacon's temple. Doubling the size of the figure solved the problem.

The Lincoln Memorial's classic white marble structure is designed in the style of a Greek temple but with its entrance on the east side instead of at either end. Carved on the walls are the Gettysburg Address and Lincoln's Second Inaugural Address. The 36 marble columns represent the states of the Union at the time of Lincoln's death, and the names of these states are carved on the frieze above the columns. The names of the 48 states in the Union when the memorial was completed in 1922 are carved on the walls above the frieze. A plaque honoring the subsequent entry of Alaska and Hawaii is in the approach plaza.

On the day of dedication, May 30, 1922, more than 50,000 people arrived for the ceremonies. Among the notables was Robert Todd Lincoln, the only surviving son of the president. Since that day, the memorial has become a national forum—the setting for celebrations, for the airing of grievances, and for commemorations.

www.nps.gov/linc

CONSTITUTION GARDENS

Washington, D.C.

On the north side of the Lincoln Memorial reflecting pool, landscaped gardens, meandering footpaths, and a lake have replaced temporary office buildings that stood here for over 50 years. Dedicated in 1976, Constitution Gardens serves as an oasis within the bustling city for visitors, residents, and wildlife. A memorial island in the middle of an artificial lake has a circle of stones bearing the names and signatures of the 56 men who signed the Declaration of Independence. Their pledge to freedom exists as a living tribute within this natural setting celebrating the U.S. Constitution.

www.nps.gov/coga

THE NATIONAL MALL & MEMORIAL PARKS RADIO STATION

The National Mall & Memorial Parks Traveler Information Station, 1670 AM, premiered in December 2006 and provides general park information, historical facts, and notice about current and special events to the millions of visitors who visit the National Mall & Memorial Parks each year. The radio station gives the listener a general orientation to available park resources such as transportation information, scheduled interpretive programs, and instruction on acquiring Washington Monument tickets. Tune in for continuously updated information.

VIETNAM VETERANS MEMORIAL

Washington, D.C.

The Vietnam Veterans Memorial Fund Inc. was incorporated April 27, 1979, to establish a memorial to those men and women who served and died during the Vietnam War. The members of the fund wished to create a memorial that would be contemplative in character, that would harmonize with its surroundings, that would contain the names of all who died or remain missing, and that would make no political statement about the war. Money was raised from private groups and individuals to finance the design and construction of the memorial; no public funds were used. Maya Ying Lin, who in 1981 was an architecture student at Yale University, won the design competition.

Built of polished black granite, the memorial is set into the ground in the form of a "V" with one arm pointing toward the Lincoln Memorial and the other toward the Washington Monument. The names are in the order of the date of the casualty, starting from the first deaths in 1959 until the last deaths in 1975. Altogether, 58,249 names of American dead and missing are inscribed on the memorial walls.

The memorial was dedicated November 13, 1982. Two years later, Frederick Hart's Three Servicemen Statue joined a flagpole bearing the military service seals near the entrance to the Wall. On November 11, 1993, the Vietnam Women's Memorial statue, sculpted by Glenna Goodacre, was added to the site to honor all the women who served. More recently, in 2004, the In Memory Plaque was dedicated to memorialize men and women who later died from causes related to the war.

www.nps.gov/vive

Visitors to the Vietnam Veterans Memorial leave mementos of their loved ones at the wall.

KOREAN WAR VETERANS MEMORIAL

Washington, D.C.

At the Korean War Veterans Memorial, a phrase engraved in granite leaps out: "Freedom is not free." These words could have easily found a home in any of the memorials on the National Mall, as they remind us all of the personal and collective sacrifices made by Americans to preserve the principles laid down by the founding fathers at our nation's inception. It is fitting, however, that they adorn the memorial dedicated to those who served in the "Forgotten War." The Korean War (1950–1953) served notice to the world that despite a crushing victory over the Axis in World War II, the United States and the rest of the free world faced a new cadre of threats to world peace. The Korean

peninsula was divided in two, much like Germany at the end of the Second World War. Communist North Korea invaded pro-Western South Korea in the summer of 1950, with a view to unifying Korea once more. Americans were once again called to arms. For three years, the military of the United States and its United Nations allies fought to maintain South Korea's freedom. The unwelcome entrance of China, which stood behind North Korea's aggression, placed an exclamation point on the struggle, reinforcing the uphill struggle required in order to keep South Korea a free nation.

One cannot help but marvel at the amount of symbolism that is contained in the Korean War Veterans Memorial. Entering the memorial from the north, the low wall to the left contains the names of the 22 members of the United Nations alliance that banded together in 1950. To the right, a field is filled with statues depicting American troops walking uphill toward the American flag, a glowing symbol of freedom. There are 19 figures, sculpted by Frank Gaylord, representing Army, Navy, Air Force, and Marine troops. These are paired with their reflections in the opposite wall. The figures and reflections add up to 38, symbolic of the 38th parallel of latitude that separates North and South Korea. The uphill slope accentuates the struggle of war, coupled with the granite slabs and foliage in the field reinforcing the harsh landscape of Korea. As one approaches the American flag, the phrase "Freedom is not free" reflects the sacrifices American and Allied troops made during the war. Next to these words, a circular pool offers a quiet area to reflect on the war and the meaning of those four words. As you exit the memorial on the south side, the large granite wall to your left is engraved with images of actual veterans who served in the armed forces during the war. From a distance, these faces resemble the high peaks of the jagged Korean peninsula.

The memorial was dedicated in West Potomac Park on July 27, 1995, the 42nd anniversary of the armistice that closed hostilities. This unique memorial was based on a design submitted by landscape architects from Pennsylvania State University and revised by the architectural firm of Cooper-Lecky.

www.nps.gov/kowa

Found upon the memorial's sculptures and walls, the soldiers' faces take on added meaning when one considers that they were modeled after actual veterans.

Neil Estern's sculpture of Franklin Roosevelt demonstrates the president's resolve and determination to lead the nation through the rigors of economic depression and global war.

FRANKLIN DELANO ROOSEVELT MEMORIAL

Washington, D.C.

"The only thing we have to fear is fear itself." These are the words of our 32nd president, a man who truly knew the meaning of the word *courage*. Despite, at age 39, being stricken with polio and paralyzed from the waist down, he emerged as a true leader, guiding our country through some of its darkest times: the Great Depression and World War II. The FDR Memorial honors this man and his story.

President Franklin Delano Roosevelt inspired millions of Americans during some of the dark days of the 1930s and 1940s. Roosevelt spoke directly to the people. His words of 1933 still echo in the hearts of many today, "I pledge you, I pledge myself, to a new deal for the American people." This statement, along with many others, is inscribed on the walls of the memorial in Washington, D.C.

Congress established the Franklin Delano Roosevelt Memorial Commission in 1955. However, because of delays arising from disagreements about designs and fund raising, the FDR Memorial waited until 1995 to take its place alongside other major presidential monuments and memorials in the Nation's Capital. Designed by Lawrence Halprin, the memorial incorporates the work of prominent American artists Leonard Baskin, Neil Estern, Robert Graham, Thomas Hardy, and George Segal, as well as master stonecarver John Benson.

The Franklin Delano Roosevelt Memorial is one of the more expansive memorials in the nation. Yet its shade trees, waterfalls, statuary, and quiet alcoves create the feeling of a secluded garden rather than an imposing structure. Located near the famous cherry trees along the western edge of the Tidal Basin on the National Mall, this is a memorial not just to Roosevelt, but also to the era he represents.

The memorial is divided into four outdoor galleries, or rooms, one for each of FDR's terms in office. The rooms are defined by walls of red South Dakota granite and by ornamental plantings. Quotations from FDR can be found carved into the granite throughout the memorial. Water cascades and quiet pools are present throughout. Each room conveys in its own way the spirit of this great man.

Sculptures inspired by photographs depict the 32nd president. A 10-foot statue shows him in a wheeled chair. A bas-relief depicts him riding in a car during his first inaugural. At the entrance to the memorial is a prologue room where there is a statue of President Roosevelt seated in a wheelchair much like the one he actually used.

Years after Roosevelt's death, his own words call out from the walls of his memorial as if he were somehow present. Americans who know FDR only as a historical figure will recognize these words by their association with great and catastrophic events. For the many Americans who lived through the Roosevelt years, the words recall personal struggles and triumphs during 12 years that seemed like a lifetime.

www.nps.gov/frde

Allegorical figures of Vision, Labor, and Adventure tower over the figure of a seated Ericsson.

JOHN ERICSSON MEMORIAL

Washington, D.C.

A native Swede and naturalized American citizen, John Ericsson was a brilliant engineer who perfected the screw propeller and designed the famous Civil War ironclad, the USS *Monitor*. Ericsson's ship engaged the Confederate ironclad, CSS *Virginia*, in the immortal battle at Hampton Roads, Virginia, in 1862. The John Ericsson Memorial, designed by James Earle Fraser, was dedicated on May 29, 1926, with President Calvin Coolidge and a crowd of thousands in attendance. The memorial stands as a shining example of the genius and patriotism of Captain Ericsson, whose contributions toward preserving the Union cannot be understated or forgotten.

www.nps.gov/nama

GEORGE MASON MEMORIAL

Washington, D.C.

Wealthy Virginia planter; mentor to George Washington, Thomas Jefferson, and James Madison; and widower with nine children to raise, the cantankerous George Mason stood regarded by his contemporaries as perhaps the wisest man of his generation. Although he preferred domestic life to the political spotlight, Mason championed liberty during the American revolutionary period and worked to consolidate the gains from this country's struggle for independence from Great Britain.

Mason was among the five more prolific speakers during the 1787 Constitutional Convention. However, when nearly all were ready to sign the final draft of the new constitution, George Mason could not bring himself to do it—even though he knew it meant harming his long friendship with his neighbor, George Washington. In the end, Mason decried the failure of the document to forbid the importation of slaves or include a bill of rights. Mason returned to Virginia to help lead the fight against ratification of the new federal constitution. Defeated, Mason retired from public life. Just before his death, he became reconciled to the Constitution when the states ratified a list of ten amendments—the Bill of Rights.

On April 9, 2002, George Mason received recognition with a memorial on the National Mall. The George Mason Memorial celebrates the achievements of the nation's preeminent constitutionalist and champion of human rights and individual liberty. At the dedication of the memorial, Chief Justice William H. Rehnquist reminded his audience that "George Mason's contributions to the new republic were less visible, but nonetheless of great importance." The memorial's quiet setting, utilizing the flower gardens surrounding historic Fountain 4, befits the character of the man who shunned attention.

www.nps.gov/gemm

The memorial is composed of a trellis providing shade over this large bronze sculpture by Wendy Ross.

THOMAS JEFFERSON MEMORIAL

Washington, D.C.

In 1934, Congress created the Thomas Jefferson Memorial Commission. Their charge was to find a location in the Nation's Capital, develop a design, and supervise the construction of a memorial to the third president. Despite its high-minded goal, the commission encountered challenges at almost every step along the way. Of the four proposed locations—on the Mall opposite the National Archives, in Lincoln Park, on the banks of the Anacostia River, and along the Tidal Basin—the Thomas Jefferson Memorial Commission always preferred the prominent Tidal Basin location. Disagreements about the design of the memorial erupted immediately. Other opposition arose because some cherry trees had to be removed before construction could begin. Despite the opposition, eventually the memorial construction began.

On December 15, 1938, President Franklin D. Roosevelt participated in the ground-breaking ceremony, and one year later, the cornerstone was laid. On the anniversary of Jefferson's 200th birthday, April 13, 1943, the memorial was dedicated. Because of the scarcity of metal in the midst of World War II, the statue of Jefferson was made of plaster. It was replaced with a bronze statue, as originally specified, on April 25, 1947.

The Jefferson Memorial reflects the essence of the man whom it honors. The graceful, domed building is the architectural shape Jefferson used in designing his own home, Monticello, and the Rotunda of the University of Virginia. The memorial design is by John Russell Pope, whose work in Washington includes the National Archives and the National Gallery of Art, West Building. Pope died before construction began, and Otto Eggers and Daniel Higgins did the final design work. Rudulph Evans sculpted the heroic statue. Inscribed on four panels along the interior walls are selections from Jefferson's writings on liberty. The first panel contains excerpts from the Declaration of Independence. The second is from his Virginia Statute of Religious Freedom. The third is about slavery and the fourth about the need for accepting change in a democracy.

The beauty of the memorial on the banks of the Tidal Basin is heightened each spring when the Japanese cherry trees bloom. In 1909, First Lady Helen Herron Taft became interested in planting Japanese cherry trees in Potomac Park. Through the efforts of

Dr. Jokichi Takamine, the discoverer of adrenalin, the city of Tokyo presented some 3,000 flowering cherry trees to the city of Washington. Mrs. Taft and Viscountess Chinda, wife of the Japanese ambassador, planted the first two trees on March 27, 1912.

Also on the grounds are a Japanese lantern more than 300 years old and a pagoda, both given by the Japanese in honor of Commodore Matthew Perry's mission to Japan in 1854. In recent years, older trees that died have been replaced with donated trees from individual and corporate patrons.

www.nps.gov/thje

With the famous cherry blossoms framing the scene, the classical columns and dome of the Thomas Jefferson Memorial form a perfect tribute to an integral figure in American history.

PENNSYLVANIA AVENUE NATIONAL HISTORIC SITE

Washington, D.C.

The Pennsylvania Avenue National Historic Site encompasses a portion of Pennsylvania Avenue and adjacent areas between the United States Capitol and the White House. Although the avenue itself extends for seven miles from M Street in Georgetown in northwest Washington, D.C., to Prince George's County in Maryland, it is its ceremonial heart between the symbols of the legislative and executive branches of the American government that is in the historic site.

Pierre L'Enfant laid out Pennsylvania Avenue in 1791 in the original plan for the Nation's Capital. Both George Washington and Thomas Jefferson considered the wide dirt road an important feature of the new capital, Washington possibly envisioning its future appearance when he designated it a "grand avenue." Parades and processions first became associated with the thoroughfare when a group of people marched along the avenue in celebration of Jefferson's second inaugural. Presidential inaugural processions are now an established tradition on Pennsylvania Avenue, but it also serves as the setting for parades and protests of ordinary citizens.

The funeral cortege of Abraham Lincoln proceeded along Pennsylvania Avenue only weeks before the Army of the Potomac celebrated the end of the Civil War by parading along the same thoroughfare. During the depression of the 1890s, Jacob Coxey and 500 supporters marched down Pennsylvania Avenue to the Capitol demanding federal aid for the unemployed. In 1901, President McKinley rode down the avenue to the Capitol to take the oath of office for his second term of office. Six months later, his funeral cortege made the same journey.

The creation of the Pennsylvania Avenue National Historic Site represents part of an official effort to reunite the avenue with local citizens and out-of-town visitors. By the 1970s, the avenue had reached a blighted state for the second time in its history. The first instance of major deterioration occurred toward the end of the 19th century and was reversed largely by the completion of the Post Office Building at the corner of 12th Street and Pennsylvania Avenue in 1899. The emergence of the historic site followed the creation by Congress of the Pennsylvania Avenue Development Corporation in 1972 to carry out a significant revitalization of the avenue.

Today, citizens and visitors, businesses and government agencies, shops, and restaurants enliven Pennsylvania Avenue, "America's Main Street." The National Historic Site it encompasses reminds us that this stretch of the avenue now reflects George Washington's description of it as "most magnificent and most convenient."

www.nps.gov/paav

As "America's Main Street," Pennsylvania Avenue perhaps has witnessed more American history than any other street in the nation.

FORD'S THEATRE NATIONAL HISTORIC SITE

Washington, D.C.

Includes the Lincoln Museum and the House Where Lincoln Died

Ford's Theatre is a thriving cultural institution located inside a treasured cultural resource in the heart of downtown Washington, D.C. Plays in production there often contain historical themes and feature well-known national talent. The theatre receives visitors from all over the world who arrive each day to see the place where President Abraham Lincoln was shot by John Wilkes Booth on April 14, 1865. Among the original items dating back to the night of the assassination on exhibit in the theatre are a framed engraving of George Washington hung on the front of the box, the sofa from inside the presidential box, and a cane-seated chair located in one of the private boxes.

National Park Service rangers and volunteers present interpretive programs on a regular basis. Rehearsals, theatrical productions, or renovations to the historic building sometimes close the theatre. However, the house where Lincoln died remains open to the public.

The Lincoln Museum is located in the basement of Ford's Theatre. Exhibits are thematically arranged to explore the temper of the times in Civil War Washington and to explore the full story of the assassination conspiracy. The most popular exhibits include the clothes Abraham Lincoln wore, the weapons John Wilkes Booth used, and pillows used to support President Lincoln's head as he lay dying. The Lincoln Museum operates daily and usually remains open when the theatre closes for performances, rehearsals, or production-related work.

Directly across the street from Ford's Theatre is the House Where Lincoln Died. Originally the home of William and Anna Petersen and their children, the house, built in 1849, is one of the oldest historic structures still in existence in the United States. Visitors today are invited to move through three rooms recreated to look like they did the night of the assassination. Using antiques of the time and wallpaper and carpet reproduced from swatches of the originals, the home reflects what life was like in the Petersen home for the family and boarders who lived with them.

Mr. Petersen was a tailor with his own shop in the city, and Mrs. Petersen took care of running the home and tending to their children. Although this house was their personal residence, the Petersens made extra money by opening their doors to boarders—individuals or couples who paid them rent in exchange for a room and meals. One of the most famous boarders at the home was John C. Breckenridge, a member of Congress. He later became vice president under James Buchanan from 1857 to 1861.

On the night of April 14, 1865, an unconscious Lincoln was carried into the Petersen home and placed in one of their bedrooms. Soldiers were immediately posted outside the house and even up on the roof to protect the home from the crowds that jammed the street clamoring to know about the president's condition.

Mrs. Lincoln was given the front formal parlor for her use between visits to her husband's bedside. Her good friends, Miss Clara Harris, who had attended the theatre with the Lincolns, and Mrs. Elizabeth Keckley, who came to the Petersen home from her nearby residence in Washington, supported her throughout the night. A message was sent to the White House, and Robert Lincoln soon arrived to be with his mother.

Secretary of War Edwin M. Stanton commanded the use of the second front room to interview witnesses to the assassination. He directed the Army in pursuit of John Wilkes Booth, the man reported to be the assassin. He also met and talked with the many government officials who came to pay their last respects to the president.

After President Lincoln died on April 15, the Petersen family realized that their home no longer belonged to them alone. Until their deaths in 1871, both Anna and William were continually asked by a steady stream of visiting strangers to see the "room where Lincoln died." After the Petersen heirs sold the house, the second owners encountered the same disruptions to their own family.

In 1896, the Petersen House was sold to the federal government, securing for all time its place in history.

www.nps.gov/foth

EXIT ONLY
DO
NOT
ENTER

NATIONAL JAPANESE AMERICAN MEMORIAL TO PATRIOTISM DURING WORLD WAR II

Washington, D.C.

This memorial acknowledges the U.S. government's unfair treatment of Japanese Americans during the Second World War. The names of 10 detention camps, where more than 120,000 Americans of Japanese ancestry were resettled, appear on the walls of the memorial as an uncomfortable reminder of an injustice. Also honored are the more than 800 Japanese Americans who died in the service of the United States during the war. More than 30,000 Japanese Americans honorably served in the armed forces of this nation despite the internment of their friends and families.

Within the memorial are inspiring words from veterans as well as from U.S. Presidents Harry Truman and Ronald Reagan. Especially poignant are President Truman's words as he welcomed home the highly decorated Japanese American veterans in 1946: "You fought not only the enemy, but you fought prejudice—and you won." The memorial was dedicated during Veterans Day Weekend 2000.

www.nps.gov/nama

The focal point of the memorial is a sculpture of cranes, a symbol with deep significance to the Japanese, trying to break free from barbed wire.

OLD POST OFFICE TOWER

Washington, D.C.

The Old Post Office is once again a lively presence on Pennsylvania Avenue. It encloses public use space with shops and food service areas, featuring cultural and other public activities. Federal offices occupy the upper floors, and the Congress Bells, a bicentennial gift to the United States from Great Britain, are now installed in the tower and rung on special occasions. The Old Post Office Tower soars mightily over "America's Main Street." The National Park Service provides daily tours by glass-enclosed elevator to the Congress Bells and to the 315-foot clock tower observation deck for views of Washington, D.C.

Designed by architect Willoughby Edbrooke in the Romanesque Revival style and completed in 1899, the Old Post Office exemplified the growing strength and increasing civic grandeur of the federal government. Within 15 years, planners and builders of federal buildings shifted their attention to designs in the Neoclassical style seen in the buildings of the Federal Triangle across 12th Street NW. The Federal Triangle is bordered by Pennsylvania Avenue, Constitution Avenue, and 15th Street NW and is part of the Pennsylvania Avenue National Historic Site. It is comprised of a unified group of important and prominent federal office buildings.

"Old" came to mean obsolete, and for 75 years, the Old Post Office was threatened with demolition. Fortunately, the economics of the Great Depression and the needs of the ensuing war effort worked in the building's favor, at least temporarily. Decades later, when a presidential commission recommended that it be torn down to complete the Federal Triangle, with only its clock tower remaining as a reminder of the past, friends of the Old Post Office organized themselves into a preservation group. Nancy Hanks, the chairman of the National Endowment of the Arts, strove to save old buildings and convinced Congress to pass the Cooperative Building Use Act in 1976. The Cooperative Use law permitted private businesses to occupy the same space as government agencies and opened the way for the adaptive reuse of the Old Post Office Building on display today.

www.nps.gov/opot

The tower's massive and antiquarian proportions perfectly illustrate the Romanesque Revival architectural style.

THE ELLIPSE

Washington, D.C.

This park area, just south of the White House, is the site of activities ranging from softball and soccer games to First Amendment demonstrations and the annual Lighting of the National Christmas Tree. It contains the broad open Ellipse, Second Division Memorial, the Boy Scout Memorial, the Zero Milestone Marker, the Haupt Fountains, and two gatehouses that once stood on the U.S. Capitol grounds. Nearby are Sherman Park and the First Division Monument area.

THE WHITE HOUSE

Washington, D.C.

The White House has been the official residence of every American president except George Washington. The first floor contains the great state rooms—East, Green, Blue, Red, and State Dining—in which the presidents entertain their guests. The second and third floors contain the private quarters for the presidents and their families. Of the state rooms, which are open free and regularly to the public (the only residence of a head of state to be readily accessible in the world), the largest is the East Room. It was intended by architect James Hoban to be a "public reception room" and has often served that function. Seven presidents who died in office have lain in state here.

The Gilbert Stuart portrait of George Washington that Dolley Madison saved before the British burned the White House in 1814 hangs here. Thomas Jefferson used the Green Room as his dining room, and today the furnishings are in the style of the later Federal period, 1800–1810. Most of the furniture was made by the famous New York cabinetmaker Duncan Phyfe. The elliptical Blue Room is decorated in the French Empire style introduced by

James Monroe in 1817 when refurnishing the rebuilt White House. Seven chairs and one sofa are original to the Monroe suite of furniture. The Red Room furniture is of the American Empire style, 1810–1830. The State Dining Room can accommodate as many as 140 persons for a formal dinner. Carved in the mantel is John Adams's hope for the White House and its occupants: "I Pray Heaven to Bestow the Best of Blessings on THIS HOUSE and on All that shall hereafter Inhabit it. May none but Honest and Wise Men ever rule under this Roof."

THE OVAL OFFICE

Alone, the words conjure up a host of images. On the one hand, the term is almost synonymous with "White House." On the other, it denotes the president at work, functioning as the chief executive of the nation. Here the work of the presidency takes place; here the president meets with advisers, determining policy and courses of action, working out a legislative program, and sometimes speaking to the nation.

Though well known, the term "Oval Office" is a 20th-century creation. Thomas Jefferson had used what is now the State Dining Room as his office. Beginning under John Quincy Adams, the offices shared the second floor with the private quarters, an arrangement that remained until the time of Theodore Roosevelt when the demands for more space by the presidential staff and by the family collided. As part of a 1902 renovation of the state floor and second floor, a "temporary" structure—the West

Wing—was erected to contain the offices of Roosevelt's staff and the Cabinet Room.

An office for the president also was created, but Roosevelt seldom used it. Seven years later, the wing was enlarged for William Howard Taft, and a new presidential office was created to imitate the original oval rooms in the residence. On Christmas Eve in 1929, this "Oval Office" and most of the West Wing were destroyed by fire; they were rebuilt the next year. In 1934, the West Wing was greatly enlarged to meet the needs for the even larger staff that President Franklin D. Roosevelt assembled. With some small changes, this is the West Wing and Oval Office in use today. Many presidents have chosen to use the desk that Queen Victoria presented to Rutherford B. Hayes. It is made from the timbers of HMS *Resolute*, a British ship rescued from the polar pack ice by American whalers.

THE RESIDENCE OF THE PRESIDENT

James Hoban, an architect born and trained in Ireland, designed the White House. The house, built of Virginia (Aquia) sandstone painted white, is in the style of an Irish Georgian country house. It is the oldest public building in the District of Columbia, its cornerstone having been laid October 13, 1792, almost one year before a similar ceremony for the Capitol building.

The White House was barely finished before remodeling began, with practically every subsequent president contributing something. Jefferson, who under a pseudonym had unsuccessfully submitted a design for the residence, added the terraces. Andrew Jackson piped in running water. Franklin Pierce installed a central heating system and the first indoor family bathroom. Rutherford B. Hayes installed the first telephone, James A. Garfield the first elevator. Benjamin Harrison brought in electricity. Herbert Hoover introduced air conditioning in the West Wing. Despite all these technological improvements, the greatest changes came during three periods of serious construction: the first after the British burned the White House in 1814; the second when the state rooms were remodeled in 1902; and the third during the renovation of 1948–1952.

Only the walls were left standing after the British burned the structure during their brief occupation of Washington (as shown in the black-and-white engraving of British troops in the city and in the 1816 watercolor with St. John's Church in the foreground). James Hoban, the original architect, supervised the rebuilding, which was completed in September 1817, early in James Monroe's administration. In 1902, the Theodore Roosevelt renovation included the enlarging of the State Dining Room and the moving of the offices to the new West Wing. In 1948, a survey revealed serious structural disrepair, so the Trumans moved across the street to Blair House for over three years. The interior was gutted, a new two-story basement was excavated, new foundations were laid, a framework was erected, and a house full of modern conveniences was rebuilt to largely the same historic floor plan. Jacqueline Kennedy helped make the White House not just an official residence but also a museum, by initiating the ongoing collecting of important examples of the fine arts and decorative arts for the public and private spaces. Spanning four administrations (1980–1996), an exterior stone restoration project included the removal of more than 30 layers of paint and the repairing of the stone of America's most renowned residence.

Public tours of the White House are available. United States citizens must submit requests through one's member of Congress, and foreign nationals should submit their requests through their respective embassies. These requests may be made up to six months in advance and should be submitted as early as possible since a limited number of tours are available.

www.nps.gov/whho

LAFAYETTE PARK

Washington, D.C.

In the center of the park is a magnificent bronze equestrian statue of Andrew Jackson by renowned sculptor Clark Mills. At the corners of the park are statues of Thaddeus Kosciuszko, Baron von Steuben, the Comte de Rochambeau, and the Marquis de Lafayette. The bench where Bernard Baruch, adviser to presidents, sat is also marked. The four cannon at the base of the Jackson statue were captured from the Spanish at the Battle of Pensacola in May 1818.

www.nps.gov/whho

FREDERICK WILLIAM AVG-
VSTVS HENRY FERDINAND
THE GREAT OF PRVSSIA
HE OFFERED HIS SWORD
ED MAJOR GENERAL AND
INSPECTOR GENERAL IN
THE CONTINENTAL ARMY
HE GAVE MILITARY TRAIN-
ING AND DISCIPLINE TO
WHO ACHIEVED THE IN-
DEPENDENCE OF THE
UNITED STATES
M·C·M·X

Beyond THE MONUMENTS

Exploring Greater Washington National Parks

Fort Stevens, Washington, D.C.

beyond monuments

Snake in log, Rock Creek Park, Washington, D.C.

Quantico Creek, Prince William Forest Park, Virginia

Kenilworth Park and Aquatic Gardens, Washington, D.C.

Trail, Turkey Run Park, George Washington Memorial Parkway, McLean, Virginia

ROCK CREEK PARK

Washington, D.C.

Rock Creek Park provides a place of recreation, interaction with nature, solitude, and a place for spiritual refreshment. It is a calm and relaxing green island that is easily and quickly accessible to a large and growing urban population. It offers an escape from tall buildings and asphalt landscape to trees and the rolling terrain of the Rock Creek Valley. It is carpeted with a splendid tapestry of natural vegetation and native flora. Rock Creek Park offers recreational opportunities to everyone from an intense and extremely diverse metropolitan area—our Nation's Capital.

The features that are administered by Rock Creek Park include numerous additional sites and parks that radiate out from the Rock Creek Valley. Collectively, the sites and landscape of Rock Creek Park reflect the diversity of reasons for creating parks. These reasons range from the need to provide visitors with sites for exercising and communing with nature, to memorializing and contemplating people and events in history that have influenced the culture of this nation. The park offers opportunities to learn about and ponder the area's 5,000-year human history; to explore and gain an appreciation of native plant and wildlife; and to develop an understanding of environmental issues and the importance of the National Park System in preservation.

Because of the park's diversity of resources and its proximity to the Nation's Capital, Rock Creek Park serves as an ambassador of the national park idea.

www.nps.gov/rocr

THE OLD STONE HOUSE

Washington, D.C.

In the midst of Washington, D.C., a city of grand memorials to national leaders and significant events, stands an unassuming building commemorating the daily lives of ordinary Americans who made this city, and this nation, unique. The Old Stone House, one of the oldest known structures remaining in the Nation's Capital, is a simple 18th-century dwelling built and inhabited by common people.

Its beautiful English garden is a popular and restive oasis in the busy shopping district of Georgetown. The house itself is a popular museum of the everyday life of middle class colonial America.

www.nps.gov/olst

MERIDIAN HILL PARK

Washington, D.C.

Meridian Hill Park is located in northwest Washington, D.C., and is bordered by 16th, Euclid, 15th, and W streets. This 12-acre Renaissance and Italian garden–inspired site was designated a National Historic Landmark in the Designed Landscape category in 1994. It is "an outstanding accomplishment of early 20th-century Neoclassicist park design in the United States." Construction of the park began in 1914 but was not finished until 1936. In 1933, the grounds were given to the National Park Service. However, the park's history predates its construction. In 1819, John Porter erected a mansion on the grounds and called it "Meridian Hill" because it was on the exact longitude of the original District of Columbia milestone marker. John Quincy Adams moved to this mansion when he left the White House in 1829. During the years of the Civil War, Union troops encamped on the park grounds. Today, while visiting the park, you can see a variety of statues and a beautiful European-style landscape. The large cascading fountain is one of the largest fountains in North America. You can also view the memorial to President James Buchanan and the statues of Dante, Joan of Arc, and Serenity.

www.nps.gov/mehi

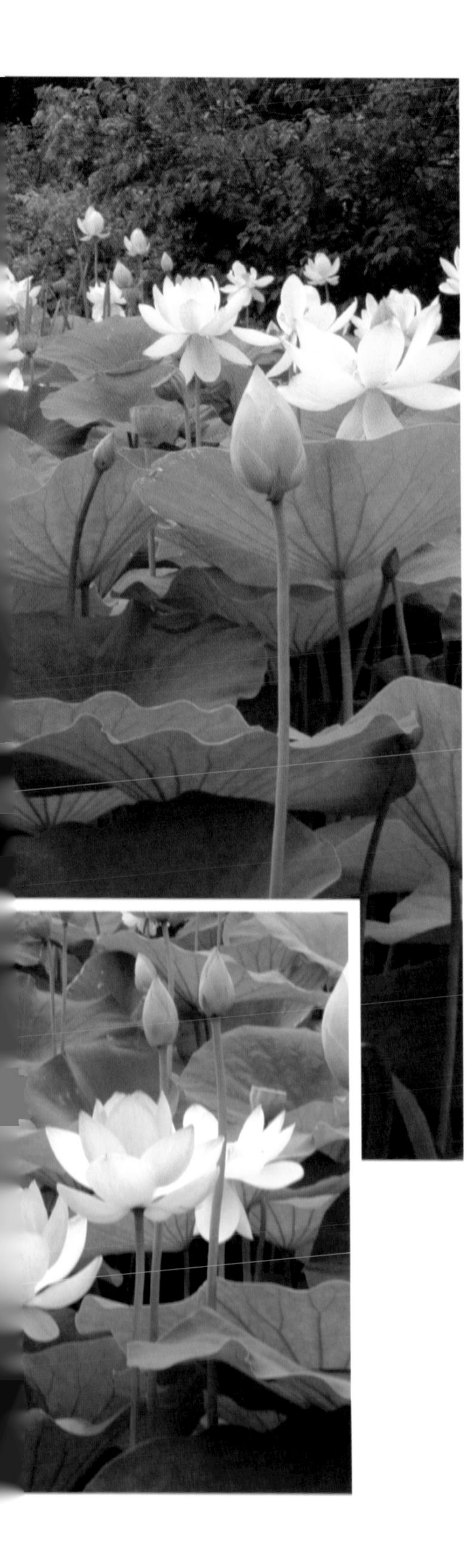

KENILWORTH PARK AND AQUATIC GARDENS

Washington, D.C.

What happens when your passion becomes your career? For Walter B. Shaw, it meant the development of the W. B. Shaw Lily Ponds along the east bank of the Anacostia River. In the early 1800s, the recently married Walter Shaw purchased 30 acres of land along the Anacostia River from his in-laws. What started with a few water lilies imported from his home state of Maine in 1882 blossomed into a commercial nursery. For 26 years, Walter Shaw and his daughter, Lucy Helen Fowler, dredged, filled, and groomed the low-lying wetlands to develop special ponds for growing and displaying the exotic plants. The Shaw gardens gained a reputation for the development, propagation, and sales of aquatic plants, especially water lilies and lotus plants.

Visit the original Shaw greenhouses and display ponds with tropical and hardy water lilies, lotus, and other plant species. The best time to view the water plants in bloom is late May through early September. Stroll the paths at this 12-acre site and enjoy the tranquil setting. You can also explore the 70 acres of protected freshwater tidal marsh, which is all that remains of the original wetlands of the Washington area. An on-site visitor center and bookstore can help you plan your visit.

www.nps.gov/keaq

Anacostia Park in Washington, D.C.
Photo by Robert Epstein

ANACOSTIA PARK

Washington, D.C.

Visit the shores of the Anacostia River to relax and rejuvenate your spirit. Whether you prefer active recreation like softball, roller-skating, and kayaking or more passive pleasures like birdwatching, strolling, and kite flying, you can find it here.

The Anacostia River's rich history of providing a refuge from the hectic hustle of urban life has attracted visitors to its shores for decades. Generations of families have gathered for picnics, enjoying the cool river breezes on a hot summer afternoon. The Anacostia Skating Pavilion has long been a meeting place for outdoor roller-skating enthusiasts. Ball fields and tennis courts are managed by the National Park Service in partnership with the District of Columbia Recreation and Parks Department and provide scenic locations for competitive sports. Launch a canoe or motorboat and see a different view of eastern Washington, D.C. Nature lovers can spot migrating birds, and local fisherman might find competition from osprey fishing the river from overhead.

www.nps.gov/anac

Anacostia River
Photo by Robert Epstein

MARY MCLEOD BETHUNE COUNCIL HOUSE NATIONAL HISTORIC SITE

Washington, D.C.

The Mary McLeod Bethune Council House National Historic Site was the last official Washington, D.C., residence of Mary McLeod Bethune, renowned educator, organizer, national political leader, president of the National Association of Colored Women's Clubs, and founder of the National Council of Negro Women. It is at this site that Mary McLeod Bethune achieved her greatest national and international recognition. The site was the first headquarters of the National Council of Negro Women where Bethune and the Council spearheaded strategies and developed programs that advanced the interests of African American women and the black community. The site is the location of the National Archives for Black Women's History, which houses the largest manuscript collection of materials solely dedicated to African American women and their organizations. Access to the archives is by appointment only. Seating is limited.

The Mary McLeod Bethune Council House NHS is a historic house museum and archives that offers a variety of programs throughout the year for every age—from guided tours and educational programs to lectures and concerts. There is limited accessibility in the house; reservations are required for groups of 10 or more. The Council House is located in the Logan Circle District of Washington, D.C.

www.nps.gov/mamc

16
1318
THE NATIONAL COUNCIL
OF
NEGRO WOMEN
Mary McLeod Bethune
NATIONAL
HISTORIC SITE
Council House

AFRICAN AMERICAN CIVIL WAR MEMORIAL

Washington, D.C.

The African American Civil War Memorial is the only national memorial to commemorate the more than 200,000 soldiers of the U.S. Colored Troops and their officers. Their names are inscribed on the Wall of Honor near the Spirit of Freedom Sculpture. The memorial is located on U Street, a historic district where many African Americans first settled during the Civil War.

The statue serves as inspiration to many, including students at nearby Howard University, which was founded in 1867. The sculpture, created by Ed Hamilton, stands 10 feet tall and features uniformed black soldiers and a sailor, protectors of the fight for freedom. On the concave inner surface of the sculpture, women, children, and elders are depicted seeking strength together as a soldier departs to fight for freedom in the war.

Eleanor Holmes Norton, Congressional Representative from the District of Columbia, introduced a bill in Congress in 1992 to establish the memorial. The African American Civil War Freedom Foundation Inc., under the leadership of Frank Smith Jr., runs the museum on the corner of 12th & U streets NW. The museum contains exhibits that explore what military life was like for African Americans who served the Union Army during the Civil War.

www.nps.gov/afam

GEORGETOWN WATERFRONT PARK

Washington, D.C.

Georgetown Waterfront Park is the largest new park in the District of Columbia since Constitution Gardens was completed in 1976. The park creates a vital final link in the 225-mile contiguous green space along the Potomac River from Mount Vernon, Virginia, to Cumberland, Maryland. The park includes open lawns and informal gardens; environmentally engineered bio-edges that preserve native plants and enhance water quality; pathways for walkers, joggers, and hikers; a bike path connecting Rock Creek Park with the Capital Crescent Trail; a labyrinth to encourage reflection and contemplation; and granite overlooks that provide scenic river views and historic images of the Georgetown waterfront.

www.nps.gov/rocr

CIVIL WAR DEFENSES OF WASHINGTON

Maryland / Virginia / Washington, D.C.

To protect the District of Columbia from Confederate assault during the Civil War, the Union Army built a complex system of field fortifications on the strategic ridges and terraces encircling the outer edges of the Federal City. The Civil War Defenses of Washington are under the jurisdiction of several national parks, including Rock Creek Park, George Washington Memorial Parkway, National Capital Parks-East, and the Potomac Heritage National Scenic Trail. The system includes Forts Mahan, Chaplin, Dupont, Davis, Stanton, Carroll, Greble, and Foote, Battery Ricketts, and various land parcels, including Shepherd Parkway, which connects all of these sites.

Today, these areas preserve the remains of the defense sites that effectively deterred the invasion of the Nation's Capital during the Civil War. They also protect significant natural corridors that contain mature native hardwood forest, geologic and aquatic resources, and a diversity of habitat for indigenous flora and fauna. This protected parkland enhances the aesthetics of the Nation's Capital and the quality of life for its citizens. Visitors to the Fort Circle Parks can enjoy a seven-mile hiking and biking trail that connects Fort Mahan to Fort Stanton, as well as recreational fields and courts, an ice-skating rink, community gardens, and picnic areas in Fort Dupont Park. At Fort Foote, two Rodman cannons are on display, and wayside exhibits help explain the site's significance.

www.nps.gov/cwdw

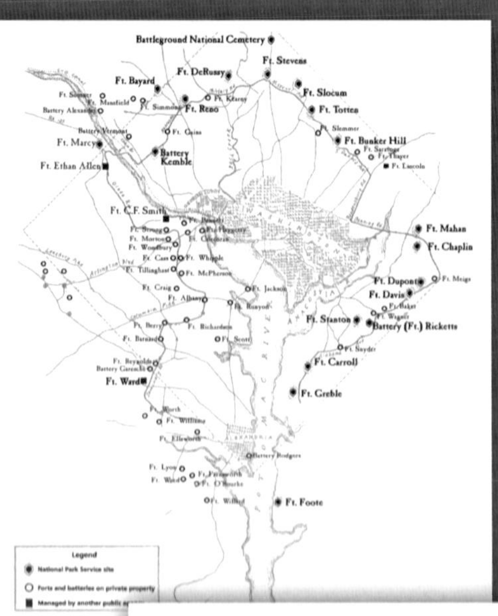

Battleground National Cemetery
Ft. Stevens
Ft. DeRussy
Ft. Bayard
Ft. Slocum
Ft. Kearny
Ft. Reno
Ft. Totten
Ft. Mansfield
Battery Alexander
Ft. Gaines
Slemmer
Ft. Bunker Hill
Battery Vermont
Ft. Marcy
Battery Kemble
Ft. Thayer
Ft. Lincoln
Ft. Ethan Allen
Ft. C.F. Smith
Ft. Strong
Ft. Morton
Ft. Woodbury
Ft. Mahan
Ft. Chaplin
Ft. Cass
Ft. Whipple
Ft. Tillinghast
Ft. McPherson
Ft. Dupont
Ft. Meigs
Ft. Craig
Ft. Jackson
Ft. Davis
Ft. Albany
Ft. Runyon
Ft. Baker
Ft. Stanton
Battery (Ft.) Ricketts
Ft. Berry
Ft. Richardson
Ft. Barnard
Ft. Scott
Ft. Snyder
Ft. Reynolds
Ft. Carroll
Ft. Ward
Ft. Greble
Ft. Worth
Ft. Williams
Ft. Ellsworth
ALEXANDRIA
Battery Rodgers
Ft. Lyon
Ft. Ward
Ft. O'Rourke
Ft. Willard
Ft. Foote
Legend
National Park Service site
Forts and batteries on private property

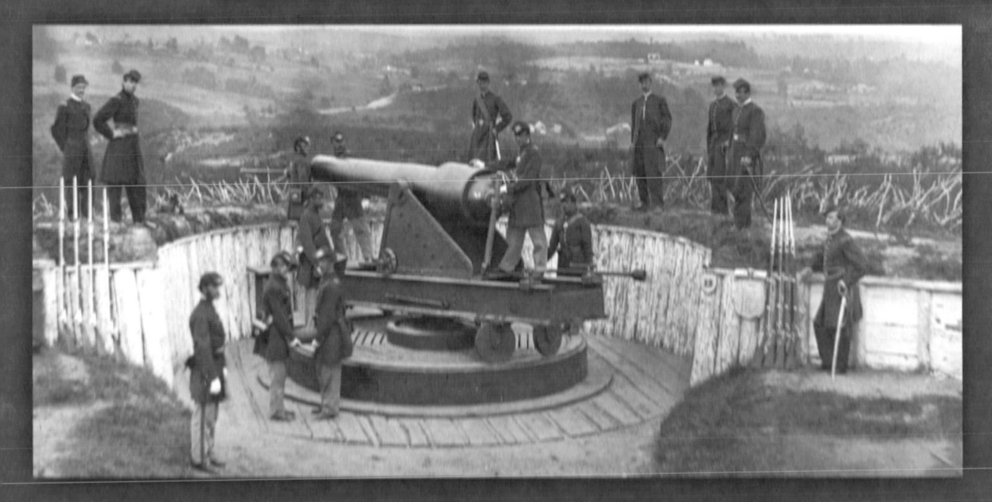

ANTIETAM NATIONAL BATTLEFIELD

Sharpsburg, Maryland

Antietam National Battlefield is preserved because of the unparalleled deadly fighting that occurred here. Antietam was the bloodiest one-day battle of the American Civil War with almost 23,000 soldiers killed, wounded, or missing. Fought on September 17, 1862, this was the culmination of Confederate General Robert E. Lee's first attempt to carry the war into Northern territory. Lee's Army of Northern Virginia challenged Union General George B. McClellan's Army of the Potomac. Furious combat raged throughout the day at such landmarks as Miller's Cornfield, Dunker Church, Sunken Road, and the Burnside Bridge. Although the battle was a tactical draw, it was a strategic Union victory as Confederates withdrew to Virginia the day after the battle. In addition, it allowed President Lincoln to issue the Emancipation Proclamation, which gave the war a dual purpose: to preserve the Union and to end slavery.

Today, visitors can explore the battlefield along the eight-mile driving tour or by hiking one of several trails. Visitors are welcome to walk through the Antietam National Cemetery as well as visit the National Museum of Civil War Medicine's Pry House Field Hospital Museum. The Antietam Visitor Center features a museum, two films, various ranger-guided programs, and a museum store. National Park Service staff take great pride in preserving and restoring the historic landscape, resulting in one of the nation's most pristine and solemn Civil War battlefields.

www.nps.gov/anti

MONOCACY NATIONAL BATTLEFIELD

Monocacy, Maryland

Monocacy National Battlefield provides a setting that has changed little since the time of the Civil War. It was the scene of the July 9, 1864, battle where Confederate forces under Lieutenant General Jubal Early advanced on Union troops led by Major General Lew Wallace in an effort to storm the United States capital and threaten President Abraham Lincoln's chances for reelection. Although Wallace's men were greatly outnumbered, their defeat on the battlefield was a strategic victory in that it delayed the Confederate advance on Washington. This provided crucial time for Union reinforcements to reach the capital.

Today, visitors to the park can enjoy a relaxing, contemplative experience via auto tour or any of four walking trails. Each of these trails offers a unique opportunity to explore a portion of the battlefield history, encounter wildlife in an agrarian setting, or merely relax in a peaceful landscape near a busy urban area.

The .5-mile Gambrill Mill Trail is accessible and fun for people of all ages. An adjacent meadow and nearby pond make it great for birdwatching.

The Worthington Trail is comprised of two intersecting loop trails (1.6 and 1.9 miles, respectively). History buffs will gain great insight into battle tactics and strategy, while others will savor the flora and fauna of the woodlands and farm fields.

The 1.75-mile Thomas Farm Trail allows battlefield travelers to walk the very ground that became the "turning point" during the Battle of Monocacy.

www.nps.gov/mono

FORT WASHINGTON PARK

Fort Washington, Maryland

First-time visitors to Fort Washington Park have often been astounded by the abundance of natural, cultural, historical, and recreational resources found within this 341-acre park. Frequently described as a place that epitomizes natural beauty and timeless historical character, Fort Washington has grown from a lonely outpost to an urban park that accommodates more than 260,000 visitors annually. Located on the Maryland shore of the Potomac River just eight miles south of Washington, D.C., this park offers visitors opportunities to enjoy living history programs in the fort, environmental education programs along the beach, nature hikes on the trails, biking along the roads, group picnicking in the grove, fishing along miles of shoreline, and an endless array of other outdoor activities. There are frequent sightings of bald eagles, osprey, hawks, and falcons as well as innumerable songbirds and waterfowl. Throughout the day and especially during the early morning, you will find fox, groundhogs, deer, and other woodland creatures meandering about. The usual serenity of the park is extraordinarily captivating. There are times when you can hear the wind blowing through the trees and waves hitting the rocks near the lighthouse on Digges Point. In the spring, the fragrance and beauty of cherry blossoms, daffodils, trumpet vines, azaleas, and many other flowering shrubs, trees, and plants can be found throughout the park. The 100 or so acres of manicured lawns offer excellent opportunities for sunbathing, reading, relaxing, playing softball or volleyball, jogging, and other recreational activities.

The history of Fort Washington can be traced back to the 17th century, when the original grant for the land was secured in 1655. The family of Charles Digges purchased the tract in 1717 and erected the Warburton Manor Estate in 1729. The remains of the Digges family mansion, which was destroyed in 1819, are located northeast of the old fort adjacent to the main parking lot where the remains of this two-story mansion are buried under three feet of dirt and grass.

President George Washington first recognized the need for placing a fort on Digges Point in 1794. This first fort, Fort Warburton, guarded the channels of the Potomac River from 1808 to 1814. On August 20, 1814, five heavily armed British warships appeared downstream from the fort, and Captain Samuel Dyson, commander of a small garrison of 60 men, ordered the fort destroyed to prevent its capture by the British during the War of 1812.

The present "old fort" named for President George Washington was constructed between 1814 and 1824, with extensive improvements and remodeling in 1848. The grounds and structures of this fort played an active role in military history up to and including World War II as a training facility for new officers and as the defender of the Nation's Capital.

This massive masonry, brick, and stone structure with its 40- to 60-foot-high walls and three-acre parade grounds, once mounted 40 cannons on the bastion and demibastion walls and in the casemates. From the late 1890s through 1922, eight concrete gun batteries were constructed as a part of the Endicott Period reinforcements to coastal defenses throughout the nation. A minefield was placed in the Potomac River near the fort to defend against submarines. During World War II, the garrison at Fort Washington grew to more than 3,000 men and women who worked and trained at what became a small city complete with a mini-rail train, pier complex, bank, bowling alley, firehouse, swimming pool, and an assortment of officers' residences, barracks, and other support buildings.

Volunteers play a significant role at the park by presenting living history programs, assisting with maintenance, and performing a variety of research and administrative functions. Throughout the spring and summer, the all-volunteer Old Guard dressed in Civil War period clothing present live cannon- and musket-firing demonstrations. Local students, scouts, and others perform an array of trail maintenance and research projects, including the construction of footbridges, picnic tables, and waysides. Many local residents have assisted the park by sharing historical images and information about relatives who actually worked or lived at the fort during its heyday.

Today, thousands of visitors frequent the park to learn about the historical defenses of Washington, to explore the trails and waterfront in search of wildlife and fishing opportunities, and to enjoy the recreational areas.

www.nps.gov/fowa

MANASSAS NATIONAL BATTLEFIELD PARK

Manassas, Virginia

Cheers rang through the streets of Washington in July 1861 as the Union Army, 34,000 strong, marched out to begin the long-awaited campaign to capture Richmond and end the war. It was an army of green recruits, few of whom had the faintest idea of the magnitude of the task facing them. The First Battle of Manassas, also known as First Bull Run, was the first major land battle of the Civil War. It was a decisive Confederate victory that dispelled all preconceived notions of a short war. The Southern victory at Second Manassas almost one year later brought the Confederacy to the height of its power and opened the way for an invasion of the North.

Set among the rolling hills of the Virginia horse country some 30 miles west of Washington, D.C., Manassas National Battlefield was twice the scene of major conflicts between Federal armies and Confederate forces. It was here on Henry Hill that General Thomas J. Jackson received his famous nickname "Stonewall" for holding his ground under tremendous artillery fire,

a site marked today by a bronze equestrian statue. Nearby is the reconstructed home of Judith Henry, an elderly widow who refused to leave her home when the fighting began, only to die from fatal injuries received during an artillery bombardment that destroyed her home.

Much of the landscape within the park still retains its wartime character. From oak-hickory forests to open meadows and farm fields dotted with worm fencing, the park is one of only a few Civil War sites that preserve a majority of the actual battlefield where troops fought and died. Historic sites include the Stone Bridge, Stone House, Dogan House, Thornberry House, and Brawner Farm. The park contains over 40 miles of recreational trails that lead visitors to historic house ruins and numerous memorial markers and monuments. Interpretive programs and historic weapons demonstrations are offered frequently in the summer and on weekends through the year.

www.nps.gov/mana

HARPERS FERRY NATIONAL HISTORICAL PARK

Harpers Ferry, West Virginia

Harpers Ferry National Historical Park, nestled in the Blue Ridge Mountains, encompasses 3,645 acres in the states of West Virginia, Maryland, and Virginia. History enthusiasts and nature lovers alike are drawn to this picturesque spot that played a significant role in our nation's past.

A visit to this quaint, historic community, at the confluence of the Potomac and Shenandoah rivers, is like stepping into the past. Stroll the brick and flagstone sidewalks. Visit exhibits and museums. Hike our trails and battlefields. The Appalachian Trail and C&O Canal converge here. Harpers Ferry offers a wide variety of experiences for visitors of all ages.

George Washington built a gun factory here, and Meriwether Lewis prepared for the Lewis and Clark Expedition here. Harpers Ferry was part of John Brown's plan to end slavery and was the site where 12,500 Federal soldiers were trapped during the Civil War. Harpers Ferry experienced the breadth of the African American experience, from slavery to emancipation, education to civil rights. Here, on this ground, slaves fought oppression and realized their dream of freedom. In 1906, members of the Niagara Movement, the first organized civil rights organization, stood here and demanded full and equal civil rights for all.

Discover Harpers Ferry and see if you agree with Thomas Jefferson, whose visit here in 1783 compelled him to write, "the scene is worth a voyage across the Atlantic."

www.nps.gov/hafe

FREDERICK DOUGLASS NATIONAL HISTORIC SITE

Washington, D.C.

Frederick Douglass, the 19th century's leading African American statesman, purchased an estate overlooking Washington, D.C., in 1877. Today, Frederick Douglass National Historic Site preserves this last residence of Douglass, a place that he came to call Cedar Hill. Life here was in stark contrast to Douglass's first 20 years. Born enslaved in 1818 on a plantation in Tuckahoe, Maryland, he endured the brutalities of slavery before escaping to freedom at age 21. Douglass became an eloquent leader of the abolitionist movement, fighting for the end of slavery on the lecture circuit and through the publication of his life story in the *Narrative of the Life of Frederick Douglass* (1845) and *My Bondage and My Freedom* (1855). After the Civil War, he held several prominent government positions and continued to fight for civil rights for all people. Douglass died in 1895 at Cedar Hill.

In 1962, the house and nine of the original 15 acres of the estate became part of the National Park System. Restored to its mid-1890s appearance, the house is furnished much as it was during Douglass's lifetime. Each room at Cedar Hill contains items from Douglass's public life, his personal belongings, and gifts from well-known people.

www.nps.gov/frdo

PRICE, BIRCH & CO.
DEALERS IN SLAVES.

NATIONAL UNDERGROUND RAILROAD NETWORK TO FREEDOM

United States

The National Underground Railroad Network to Freedom Act of 1998 directs the National Park Service (NPS) to establish a program that tells the story of resistance to the institution of slavery in the United States through escape and flight. This story illustrates a basic founding principle of this nation, that all human beings embrace the right to self-determination and freedom from oppression. Through the National Underground Railroad Network to Freedom Program, the NPS is demonstrating the significance of the Underground Railroad, not only in the eradication of slavery, but also as a cornerstone of our national civil rights movement.

The program coordinates preservation and education efforts nationwide, and is working to integrate local historical sites, museums, and interpretive programs associated with the Underground Railroad into a mosaic of community, regional, and national stories. One of the principal objectives of the program is to validate the efforts of local and regional organizations, and make it easier for them to share expertise and communicate with the NPS and each other.

There are three main components to the program:

- Educating the public about the historical significance of the Underground Railroad;

- Providing technical assistance to organizations that identify, document, preserve, and interpret sites, travel routes, and landscapes related to the Underground Railroad, or operate interpretive or educational programs or facilities; and

- Developing a network of sites, programs, and facilities with verifiable associations to the Underground Railroad.

Much of the historic physical evidence of places—the buildings and landscapes—important to the Underground Railroad have been altered or destroyed. It is necessary to recognize commemorative and interpretive efforts, in addition to identifying and preserving the sites that remain. Through its definition of the Underground Railroad, the program seeks to focus attention on those seeking freedom.

www.cr.nps.gov/ugrr

GEORGE WASHINGTON MEMORIAL PARKWAY

Maryland / Virginia / Washington, D.C.

The George Washington Memorial Parkway is the "Road to Adventure," a national park featuring more than 25 different park sites, most of which are connected by a planned, landscaped road. The park's configuration links various places associated with George Washington's life and the development of the nation. It protects and preserves natural scenery and

habitats, and provides recreational opportunities along the Potomac River.

George Washington Memorial Parkway is a landmark in the history of American park development and highway design. The first segment, originally called the Mount Vernon Memorial Highway, extended from Memorial Bridge to Mount Vernon. Completed in 1932 to commemorate the bicentennial of George Washington's birth, the Mount Vernon Memorial Highway was widely praised for its blend of modern engineering, landscape architecture, historic preservation, and patriotic sentiment. Later development of the parkway included extensions from Memorial Bridge to the Capital Beltway, as well as the Clara Barton Parkway in Maryland.

Stunning views of the Potomac River can be seen throughout parkway sites at Great Falls Park and along the Potomac Heritage Trail, a 10-mile foot trail from Theodore Roosevelt Island parking lot to near the American Legion Bridge. People may walk, ride a bike, jog, or rollerblade from near Theodore Roosevelt Island to the edge of Mount Vernon along the 18.5-mile multiuse Mount Vernon Trail. Or, they may take a short walk at Dyke Marsh Wildlife Preserve.

In addition, the parkway includes unparalleled locations to explore history and experience recreational opportunities. At Arlington House, the Robert E. Lee Memorial, speak with a ranger about the Custis, Lee, and Washington family histories. Attend a tour of Clara Barton House and learn about Barton's lifelong passion for helping others and the development of the American Red Cross. Ride on a carousel, attend a puppet show, visit a children's museum, go to a dance, sign up for an art class, or attend a ranger-led program about the civil rights movement at Glen Echo Park. Ponder the meanings of freedom, honor, valor, bravery, integrity, and leadership while visiting the U.S. Marine Corps War Memorial (commonly known as the "Iwo Jima Memorial"). Learn about the legacies of the 26th president of the United States at Theodore Roosevelt Island or the 36th president at Lyndon Baines Johnson Memorial Grove.

With more than 25 different sites to explore, the George Washington Memorial Parkway provides something for everyone.

www.nps.gov/gwmp

DYKE MARSH WILDLIFE PRESERVE

Virginia

Listen to the birds sing, watch an osprey build a nest, take a great nature photo, see a marsh flower in bloom, or enjoy a short hike to an overlook by the Potomac River at Dyke Marsh Wildlife Preserve. Regardless of the recreational activity, the marsh provides people with the opportunity to "soothe their souls" with peace and quiet in a busy urban area.

Yet, human interactions with Dyke Marsh have not always been so peaceful. In the early 1800s, colonial farmers "diked" or built earthen walls around the perimeter of the marsh in order to create more "fast" or dry land not inundated by the high tides. This land was used to grow crops or graze livestock.

For a long time, wetlands were considered wastelands in the United States. In the 1930s, construction scrap was heaped onto the wildlife acreage. In the 1950s and 1960s, a company dredged in Dyke Marsh to remove sand and gravel. In the mid-1970s, when discussion started about possible dumping of dredged river spoil into the marsh, a group of local naturalists decided to form a nonprofit organization to cooperate with the National Park Service in promoting the well-being of the marsh.

Today, Dyke Marsh is much different than it was just 50 years ago. It is estimated that Dyke Marsh once consisted of 650 acres; now it is 380 acres in size. Yet, despite its limited size, Dyke Marsh provides critical habitat for a diverse array of animals, including brown bats, red foxes, bullfrogs, northern water snakes, and snapping turtles. Plants in the marsh include cattail, arrow arum, spatterdock, and joe-pye weed.

www.nps.gov/gwmp

FORT HUNT PARK

Virginia

The sights and sounds of picnickers, joggers, and walkers camouflage the history of Fort Hunt Park. Because of its proximity to the Nation's Capital, just 11 miles south of Washington, D.C., what occurred on this site frequently mirrored the political, social, and military history of the United States. From the colonial era to the present, this site was used as farmland (including part of George Washington's River Farm), a Spanish-American War coastal fortification, a Civilian Conservation Corps camp, and the setting for top-secret World War II military intelligence operations.

Today, visitors may view on-site exhibits tracing the history of Fort Hunt. In addition, people may reserve large group picnic areas from April to October or use smaller, non-reservable picnic areas year-round. Other activities available include ranger-led programs (year-round) and a concert series (summer).

www.nps.gov/gwmp

AIRMEN of NOTE

LYNDON BAINES JOHNSON MEMORIAL GROVE

Washington, D.C.

Lyndon Baines Johnson Memorial Grove honors the legacy of the 36th president of the United States. Built with private funds, this 17-acre memorial park was dedicated on April 6, 1976, in Lady Bird Johnson Park, on an island in the Potomac River in Washington, D.C. Designed by landscape architect Meade Palmer, the grove consists of two sections. In the first section, a megalith of pink granite is surrounded by four granite tablets inset in the plaza with quotations from Johnson's speeches. A serpentine pattern of trails extends throughout the grove. The second area, a grassy meadow, provides a tranquil refuge for reflection and rejuvenation. Trails and occasional benches are shaded by hundreds of white pine and dogwood trees and are beautifully framed by azaleas and rhododendrons.

www.nps.gov/gwmp

THEODORE ROOSEVELT ISLAND

Washington, D.C.

In Washington, D.C., on a wooded island in the middle of the Potomac River, you will find a memorial to Theodore Roosevelt, the 26th president of the United States. Roosevelt's passion for the earth's natural places and his foresight for planning for their preservation contributed greatly to the conservation legacy Americans treasure today.

During his presidency, Roosevelt recognized the onset of a conservation crisis. Bison, beaver, and certain species of birds were fast disappearing, while other species had already become extinct. Approximately 80 percent of the nation's prime forests had been cut down for farms, building materials, and fuel. Years of continuous farming had taken a toll on soil fertility.

Roosevelt's leadership changed the public's misperception that America's natural resources were boundless. Under Roosevelt's leadership, the federal government expanded its role in conserving our nation's resources.

Roosevelt signed the Antiquities Act into law in 1906. This law has been used to protect magnificent cliff dwellings, ruins, and missions on public lands. Roosevelt provided public protection for nearly 230 million acres of land in the United States during his tenure in office. He created 18 national monuments, five national parks, 150 national forests, 51 federal bird reservations, and four national game reserves. Several monuments later became part of the National Park Service, including Devil's Tower, Lassen Volcanic, Muir Woods, and the Grand Canyon. He established the U.S. Forest Service.

Roosevelt also made many other contributions. His presidential legacies include supporting women's and civil rights, starting

construction of the Panama Canal, and participating in negotiations to put an end to the Russo-Japanese War.

Theodore Roosevelt Island is a quiet place to remember his legacy. This is a place where visitors can take a "nature break" just as Theodore Roosevelt often did in natural areas around the world during his lifetime. Listen to the birds, observe a turtle sunning itself, and see what's flowering near the boardwalk.

Visitors can learn about the diverse history of the island, too, including Native American use of it as a seasonal fishing village. George Mason IV, author of the Virginia Declaration of Rights, owned the island. The Mason family ran a ferry from its shores and son John built a mansion here in the 1790s. During the Civil War, the site served as a training area for the Union Army, including the "First U.S. Colored Troops."

www.nps.gov/this

THEODORE
ROOSEVELT

UNITED STATES MARINE CORPS WAR MEMORIAL

Virginia

In a fraction of a second and one click of a camera, news photographer Joe Rosenthal captured a powerful image of the second flag raising during the Battle of Iwo Jima on February 23, 1945. This image captivated a war-weary nation and fueled its resolve to push for victory in World War II. The United States Marine Corps War Memorial, inspired by and based upon this Pulitzer Prize–winning photograph, is a testament to the bravery, honor, and sacrifices of the U.S. Marine Corps in its long and celebrated history since 1775.

Sculptor Felix W. de Weldon found Rosenthal's photograph so inspirational that he immediately began sculpting a wax model of the scene. After sculpting two nine-foot-tall versions for a war bond drive, de Weldon was commissioned to sculpt the present 78-foot-high U.S. Marine Corps War Memorial.

On the memorial, six figures (five Marines and one Navy corpsman) stand upon a jumble of igneous rock that represents volcanic debris on Mount Suribachi. Atop the memorial, the six figures are depicted raising a flag on a 60-foot pole. Today, a flag flies from this location 24 hours a day as per a presidential proclamation. Inscribed on the base of the memorial is a tribute by Fleet Admiral Chester W. Nimitz to the fighting men on Iwo Jima: "Uncommon Valor was a Common Virtue." Below this is inscribed "*Semper Fidelis*"—Latin for "always faithful"—the motto of the United States Marine Corps. The names of major engagements involving Marines are burnished in gold at the base of the memorial.

Dedicated by President Dwight D. Eisenhower on November 10, 1954, the memorial is a symbol of our nation's gratitude to Marines who have served and sacrificed their lives for freedom. Marines, naval service members, and friends donated funds to cover the entire cost of the memorial ($850,000).

The U.S. Marine Corps War Memorial continues to hold meaning for people today, just as the original image captured the hearts and minds of Americans in 1945. Visitors are welcome to visit the memorial on their own or for special activities. Sunset Parades, featuring the Marine Drum and Bugle Corps and the Silent Drill Platoon, are held on the memorial grounds on Tuesday evenings during the summer. Performances are free; no reservations are required.

www.nps.gov/gwmp

THE NETHERLANDS CARILLON

Virginia

"So many voices in our troubled world are still unheard."

"From the People of the Netherlands to the People of the United States."

This simple dedication on the Netherlands Carillon expresses the gratitude of the Dutch people for American aid received during and after World War II. The carillon itself symbolizes the friendship between the people of the Netherlands and those of the United States—a friendship characterized by a common allegiance to the principles of freedom, justice, and democracy, which has weathered temporary differences. To that friendship and those principles, the Netherlands Carillon is dedicated.

The idea for this symbolic gift came from G. L. Verheul, a Dutch government official in The Hague. When the concept took shape, the drive for funds to build the carillon and the tower met with generous response from all sections of the Netherlands. Queen Juliana endorsed the project, and on April 4, 1952, during a visit to the United States, she presented a small silver bell to President Truman as a token of the carillon to come. In ceremonies at Meridian Hill Park in Washington, D.C., the queen spoke of the importance of the small bells of the carillon:

> To achieve real harmony, justice should be done also to the small and tiny voices, which are not supported by the might of their weight. Mankind could learn from this. So many voices in our troubled world are still unheard. Let that be an incentive for all of us when we hear the bells ringing.

During the next few years, the bells were completed and sent to Washington, D.C. In 1954, the 49-bell carillon was installed in a temporary tower in West Potomac Park, where it was formally accepted by

the United States. The present tower was built near the United States Marine Corps War Memorial, and in 1960, the bells were installed. On May 5, 1960, the 15th anniversary of the liberation of the Netherlands from the Nazis, the carillon was officially dedicated.

With the 50th anniversary of the liberation of the Netherlands to be celebrated in 1995, a group of prominent Dutch businessmen, mindful of the original motivation of the Netherlands Carillon as a token of gratitude for the American assistance in restoring Holland's freedom, decided to establish a foundation to assist in the modernization and refurbishing of the carillon and the tower. Together with the Netherlands Chamber of Commerce in the United States, and with the meaningful encouragement from the Netherland-American Foundation, they established a legal entity, Foundation Nederlands Carillon Washington D.C. 1945–1995, to raise the necessary funds that would ensure that the carillon would be completely modernized. The project, with strong financial support from the Netherlands government, moved ahead with full speed, and the 50th Bell of the Netherlands Carillon was officially dedicated on Friday, May 5, 1995, on the 50th anniversary of the liberation of the Netherlands.

The smaller bells were removed and returned to the Netherlands to be reworked. The larger bells (which would have been extremely difficult to remove) were reworked in place. The original playing console was removed and a new unit installed. The 50th bell was added to the carillon as a symbol of the 50 years of freedom enjoyed by Holland since 1945.

www.nps.gov/gwmp

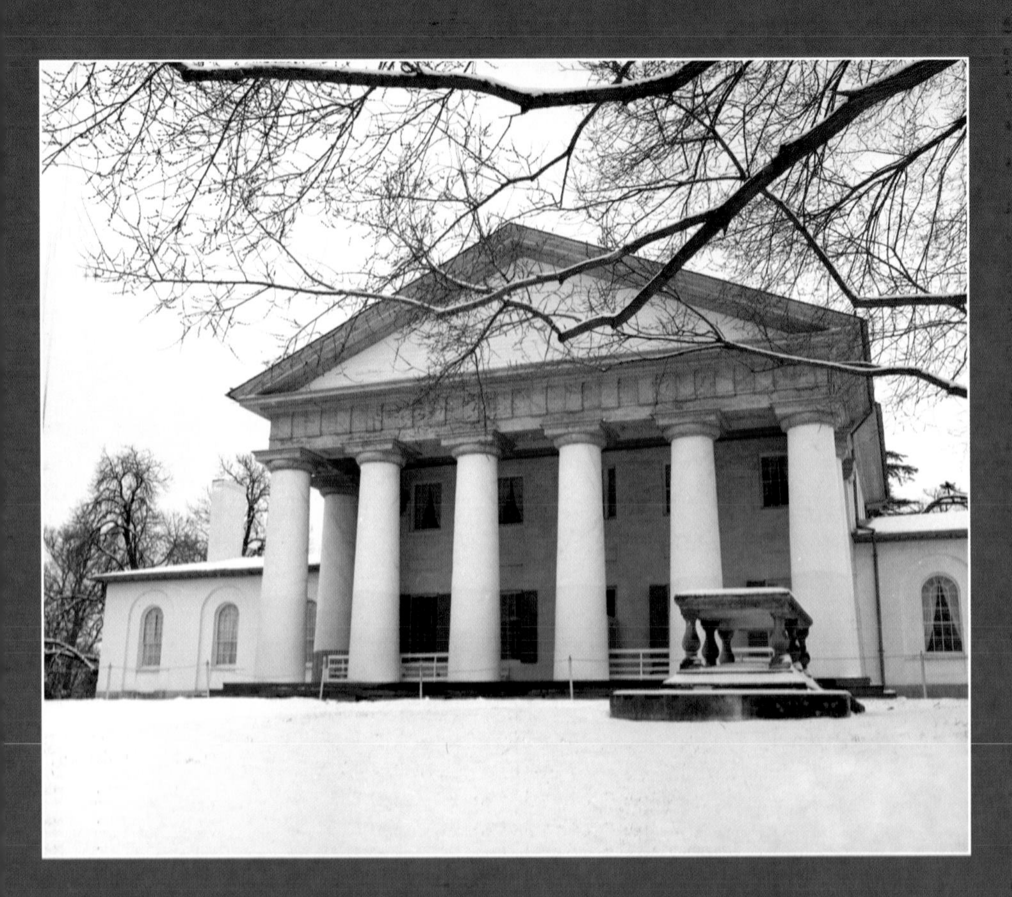

ARLINGTON HOUSE

Virginia

Arlington House, The Robert E. Lee Memorial, is located within Arlington National Cemetery and is managed by George Washington Memorial Parkway, a unit of the National Park Service. To reach the house, visitors may walk from the Arlington National Cemetery parking area (fee for parking) or ride the Tourmobile (fee for narrated shuttle).

Robert E. Lee considered Arlington House his home for 30 years. The Greek Revival mansion belonged to George Washington Parke Custis, the grandson of Martha Washington. He and his slaves built the house between 1802 and 1818. Custis and his wife, Mary Fitzhugh, had one child who survived infancy. Their daughter, Mary Anna Randolph Custis, married Robert E. Lee in 1831 at Arlington. The Lee family, which included seven children, divided its time between Arlington and Lee's army posts. When Custis died in 1857, Mrs. Lee inherited the property. In April 1861, Lee was at Arlington when he made "the most difficult decision of his life" and resigned from the U.S. Army on the eve of the Civil War. His service in the Confederacy cost the family their home. In June 1864, Arlington National Cemetery was established on the grounds of the estate.

In 1925, the house became a memorial to Lee, to recognize his efforts to reunite the country after the Civil War.

www.nps.gov/arho

ARLINGTON NATIONAL CEMETERY

Virginia

Surrounded with green slopes, Arlington National Cemetery provides shelter for many veterans from every war that has involved our nation. The grounds at Arlington National Cemetery are divided into numbered and lettered points of interest sections. The military burial grounds contain gravesites of many notable American presidents, leaders, and servicemen.

The origins of Arlington Cemetery are traced back to just before the onset of the American Civil War. George Washington Parke Custis, owner of the 1,100-acre Arlington plantation, willed the estate to his daughter, Mary. On June 30, 1831, she married a young Army officer, Robert E. Lee. Together, they lived at Arlington House for more than 30 years.

In 1861, with war between the states inevitable, Lee resigned his commission and left Arlington House when he accepted Jefferson Davis's offer rather than bear arms against his native Virginians. He left his beloved estate, never to return.

Soon after, Federal troops crossed the Potomac. The following year, the government levied a property tax on Arlington estate for the sum of $92.07. Mrs. Lee, the actual owner of the estate, sent a proxy to

pay the tax, but the government refused the money on the grounds that it had to be paid by the titleholder of the land. Consequently, Arlington House and its environs were confiscated and sold to the federal government in May 1864.

Three Union fortifications were built on the land, and 200 acres in the immediate vicinity of Arlington House were set aside as a national cemetery. On May 13, 1864, the first burials took place on the Arlington estate. By the end of the war, the rolling hillsides of the Arlington plantation were marked by the headstones of more than 7,000 soldiers.

In addition, Freedman's Village was established on the Arlington estate in June 1863. It existed for more than 30 years, providing housing, education, employment training, medical care, and food for former slaves who had migrated to the capital area. More than 3,800 blacks from Freedman's Village are buried in Section 27, their headstones marked with their names and the word "Civilian" or "Citizen."

Following the war, Lee's oldest son filed suit in federal court arguing that the government's confiscation of the land had been unconstitutional. In 1882, the Supreme Court upheld Lee's suit and awarded him $150,000, the market value of the land. The title was then formally transferred, forever ensuring Arlington's future as a national cemetery.

For the almost four million people who visit annually, Arlington National Cemetery represents many different things. For some, it is a chance to walk among headstones that chronicle American history. For many, it is an opportunity to remember and honor the nation's war heroes, and for others, it is a place to say a last farewell to family members or friends during a funeral service.

Whatever the motivation, Americans see Arlington Cemetery as our nation's most sacred shrine, an embodiment of the sacrifices made to uphold our country's ideals and freedom.

Although not the largest national cemetery in the country, Arlington is by far the most famous. There are more than 300,000 veterans and their dependents buried here on 624 acres of land. From Pierre L'Enfant, who served as George Washington's aide during the American Revolution, to General Maxwell Taylor, chairman of the Joint Chiefs of Staff during the Vietnam conflict, there are veterans buried at Arlington representing every war the United States has fought.

Funeral procession

JFK's Eternal Flame with Arlington House in background

Arlington National Cemetery with
Netherlands Carillon in background

Arlington is only one of more than 130 national cemeteries throughout the country. Unlike most of the others, which are run by the Department of Veterans Affairs, Arlington Cemetery is administered by the Department of the Army. In addition, in-ground burial regulations here are more restrictive. The purpose of the regulations is to keep Arlington an active cemetery for as long as possible. At the current rate of approximately 27 funerals daily (Monday through Friday), it is projected that the cemetery has enough space to accommodate ground burials up to the year 2060.

Arlington hosts more than 3,000 ceremonies each year, conducts more than 6,000 funerals annually, and is one of the most visited sites in Washington, D.C. Most importantly, Arlington is a testimony to the sacrifices and contributions of thousands of men and women who have made the United States what it is today.

Visitors arriving by car are advised to pay a parking fee at the visitor center parking lot, which is accessible directly off Memorial Drive. You can also reach the cemetery by using the Metro Blue Line, which is a five-minute walk along Memorial Drive to Arlington National Cemetery Visitor Center. Visitors can obtain general information about Arlington National Cemetery at the visitor center and bookshop locations.

www.arlingtoncemetery.org

Tomb of the Unknown Soldier

Sentinels keep their uniforms and weapons pristine.

Changing of the guard, mid-change with three guards

GREAT FALLS PARK

Virginia

Great Falls Park in Virginia, a unit of the George Washington Memorial Parkway, is located approximately 14 miles upstream from the Nation's Capital. This 800-acre park preserves one of the most recognizable natural landmarks in the area, the Great Falls of the Potomac. A five-minute walk from the main parking area adjacent to the visitor center offers views of the Potomac River building speed and force as it falls through a series of steep, jagged rocks and flows through the narrow Mather Gorge on its journey to the Chesapeake Bay. The Great Falls of the Potomac displays one of the steepest and most spectacular fall line rapids of any eastern river. Great Falls Park includes significant plant communities not

found elsewhere in the region, including globally rare species.

Great Falls Park also preserves the historic ruins of the Patowmack Canal. Often referred to as the engineering feat of the 18th century, the canal was one of America's first. This project of George Washington's, built between 1785 and 1802, made the river navigable west to the Ohio River Valley, with the hope of binding this new nation together in a network of trade and mutual interest.

A popular destination for local residents and international visitors, the park offers a variety of recreational activities such as rock climbing, hiking, fishing, picnicking, and biking.

www.nps.gov/grfa

GLEN E
PARI

GLEN ECHO PARK

Maryland

Glen Echo Park was originally established as a Chautauqua in 1891. (A Chautauqua was an annual educational meeting providing public lectures, concerts, and dramatic performances. The meeting was named after the first such series held in Chautauqua, New York, in 1874.) Converted to an amusement park in 1899, Glen Echo Park was one of the premier amusement parks in the Washington, D.C., area, closed in 1968 because of the lack of public transportation and the development of different forms of mass entertainment in the Washington area. Taken over by the National Park Service in 1971, the park has become a cultural arts center, a local recreational area, and a gathering place for a wide variety of cultural and ethnic groups from the metropolitan area.

The arts program at Glen Echo is managed under a cooperative agreement by the Glen Echo Park Partnership for Arts and Culture Inc. Programs include several hundred classes per year in the fine and performing arts, a dynamic social dance program, a children's environmental program, a puppet theater, a theater for children, a working pottery studio, and a variety of smaller artists' studios.

The National Park Service cosponsors a wide variety of multicultural events at the park and provides the more traditional services expected by visitors to any park in the National Park System.

From May through September, a full schedule of folk demonstrations, workshops, changing art exhibits, and evening ballroom and square dancing take place. Visit artists' workshops or sign up for classes in ceramics, dance, music, painting, and drama. Glen Echo is a community park dedicated to cultural activities similar to those fostering liberal and practical education by the early Chautauquans who established the park in 1891. Buildings with curious names and quaint facades, such as Candy Corner, Hall of Mirrors, and Spanish Ballroom, recall when Glen Echo was an amusement park and one of the most popular places in Washington. The storied Dentzel Carousel with a Wurlitzer Military 165 Band Organ still operates and is a joy to see and hear.

www.nps.gov/glec

CLARA BARTON NATIONAL HISTORIC SITE

Maryland

Clara Barton moved permanently to Glen Echo, Maryland, in 1897, after trolleys and telephone service reached the town. There she established her home, the first permanent headquarters of the American Red Cross, and the primary Red Cross storage facility in her original 1891 structure in Glen Echo. Miss Barton continued to operate the Red Cross from Glen Echo until her 1904 resignation from the organization she had founded. She continued to use the building as her home until her death in 1912.

The National Park Service opened the site in April 1975 as the first national park site dedicated to a woman and began restoring the site to its appearance during Miss Barton's residence. The restoration work is ongoing.

The site is now the focus of an active education program, as well as a source for women's history for school children in the Washington, D.C., area. The American Association of Museums has accredited the site since 1995.

www.nps.gov/clba

CLAUDE MOORE COLONIAL FARM

Virginia

Claude Moore Colonial Farm offers visitors a chance to explore an 18th-century farm at a leisurely pace. Different points of interest include the tobacco house, the farmhouse, areas where livestock are kept, the kitchen garden, and the orchard. In addition, guests may encounter members of the farm family going about their daily chores. A complete walking tour of the farm is approximately three-fourths of a mile.

A working tenant farm, Claude Moore Colonial Farm sits on a few hilly acres just a few minutes from the George Washington Memorial Parkway. Programs are announced during the planting and harvesting seasons.

The National Park Service in concert with a nonprofit group manages Claude Moore Colonial Farm.

www.1771.org

MOUNT VERNON ESTATE AND GARDENS

Virginia

Mount Vernon Estate and Gardens stretches over four acres and is only a five-minute walk south of the mansion and is adjacent to the wharf on the Potomac River. George Washington is honored at the site as the president and commander-in-chief.

Washington acquired the mansion in 1754. From 1759 until the American Revolutionary War, Washington, who at the time aspired to become a prominent agriculturist, operated the estate as five separate farms. Washington took a scientific approach to farming and kept extensive and meticulous records of both labor and results.

Following his service in the war, Washington returned to Mount Vernon. During his two terms as president of the United States (1789–1797), Washington spent 434 days in residence at Mount Vernon. After his presidency, Washington devoted much of his time to tending the expansive grounds of his estate and to the mansion. The remains of George and Martha Washington, as well as other family members, are entombed on the grounds.

Mount Vernon Estate and Gardens is open daily, with hands-on activities from April to October. The Mount Vernon Ladies' Association of the Union operates the estate. There is limited wheelchair accessibility on the grounds.

www.mountvernon.org

TRANSPORT AND TRADE—WATER VS. RAIL

THE PATOWMACK CANAL 1785–1828

After the American Revolution, merchants in eastern cities wanted to tap the western region's resources and markets. The plan for internal improvements included a navigable waterway to connect east and west. As early as 1754, George Washington envisioned a system of river and canal navigation along the Potomac River to reach the fertile Ohio Valley. Largely through his efforts, the Patowmack Company was organized in 1785 to carry out this mission. George Washington was chosen as its first president. He was frequently on the work site as canals that skirted the obstructions were constructed, channels dug, and boulders removed. The work was extremely difficult, especially at Great Falls. The lock system installed there, which gradually lowered boats down to the level of the river below the falls, has been recognized by construction experts as an engineering marvel.

To bypass the falls, rapids, and other impediments to navigation, the Patowmack Canal Company constructed five skirting canals around impassible sections of the river. Small, raft-like boats, poled by hand with the help of the river currents, carried furs, lumber, flour, and farm produce to Georgetown. Although a vast improvement over slow and cumbersome overland transport, these transportation improvements were still inadequate. Plans to build a separate, more reliable channel paralleling the Potomac River were soon put into place.

Construction of the Chesapeake and Ohio Canal began at the end of an era. On July 4, 1828, as President John Quincy Adams broke

ground just outside of Georgetown for the C&O Canal, a newer means of transportation was started in Baltimore, Maryland.

The founders of the United States, including George Washington, envisioned opening the opportunity of the western frontier through waterways. The Chesapeake and Ohio Canal was conceived to link the young Nation's Capital with the developing west by following the ancient Potomac River corridor through the Appalachian Mountains. From 1828 to 1850, a largely immigrant labor force, seeking opportunities of their own, struggled to hack the canal out of the Potomac's floodplain forests and cliffs. Their efforts resulted in a 184.5-mile canal from Georgetown to Cumberland, Maryland. However, the role of linking east with west across a continent would be achieved by the newer technology of the railroad. Even so, mule-drawn boats carried coal and other cargo on the canal until 1924.

In 1938, the federal government saw a new opportunity in the defunct canal. This time, young, impoverished men signed on to the Civilian Conservation Corps to restore a portion of the canal and create a national park. In 1954, concerned citizens shepherded by Supreme Court Justice William O. Douglas led an effort to prevent the construction of a parkway along the canal. Today, hikers and bicyclists can still enjoy Douglas's "refuge, a place of retreat, a long stretch of quiet and peace at the Capital's back door."

CHESAPEAKE AND OHIO CANAL NATIONAL HISTORICAL PARK

Great Falls, Maryland

The Great Falls of the Potomac have drawn people to the river's shore for centuries. To American Indians, it was a gathering place. To George Washington, it was an impediment to navigation. To thousands of visitors every year, it is an awe-inspiring site. The Great Falls Tavern Visitor Center continues a long tradition of hospitality for visitors to the Great Falls area of C&O Canal National Historical Park. Soon after the canal's groundbreaking in 1828, construction began on the original lock-house. In response to travelers' requests for shelter and a meal, the locktender here at Great Falls, W. W. Fenlon, asked the Canal Company to build a three-story north wing for a hotel. The hotel opened for business in 1831. Guests entered into a large, windowed room with fireplaces and a bar. As the inn's first proprietor, Mr. Fenlon presided over lively entertainment, such as fishing parties, dances, and social events in the "ballroom," in addition to good dinners and comfortable places to sleep. Exhibits in the visitor center interpret the human and natural history of this special place. Park staff and volunteers provide orientation and maps for the numerous hiking trails in the area. Hikers are advised to stick to the trail and Leave No Trace to help protect the globally rare plant communities found along this scenic area of the Potomac Gorge. Interpretive programs are presented year-round while boat rides are offered in the spring, summer, and early fall.

Canal Place Visitor Center, Cumberland

Cushwa Warehouse, Williamsport

CHESAPEAKE AND OHIO CANAL NATIONAL HISTORICAL PARK

Georgetown Terminus, Washington, D.C.

Established in 1751, Georgetown flourished as a tobacco port until the middle of the 19th century. Because of natural obstructions to transportation farther up the Potomac River, the Chesapeake and Ohio Canal began its 184.5-mile journey to the reaches of Western Maryland. Explore the beautiful architecture, rich history, and vibrant commercial life that Georgetown offers. Step back in time by riding a reproduction canal boat pulled by mules as it travels along the canal through the old warehouse district of Georgetown in the spring, summer, and early fall. Interpretive walks, talks, and bike rides are also offered on a seasonal basis. The towpath of the canal provides hikers and bicyclists with a nearly level surface to explore nature and history along the Potomac River to Cumberland, Maryland.

Cumberland Terminus, Maryland

Cumberland is the western terminus of the C&O Canal where boats were loaded with more than 110 tons of coal. Today visitors can see interactive canal exhibits at the Canal Place Visitor Center.

Williamsport, Maryland

Williamsport is a classic canal town. Near the midpoint on the C&O Canal, many boats unloaded at the Cushwa Warehouse, providing coal and other ware for the local community. The canal closed in the winter months to allow for repairs.

www.nps.gov/choh

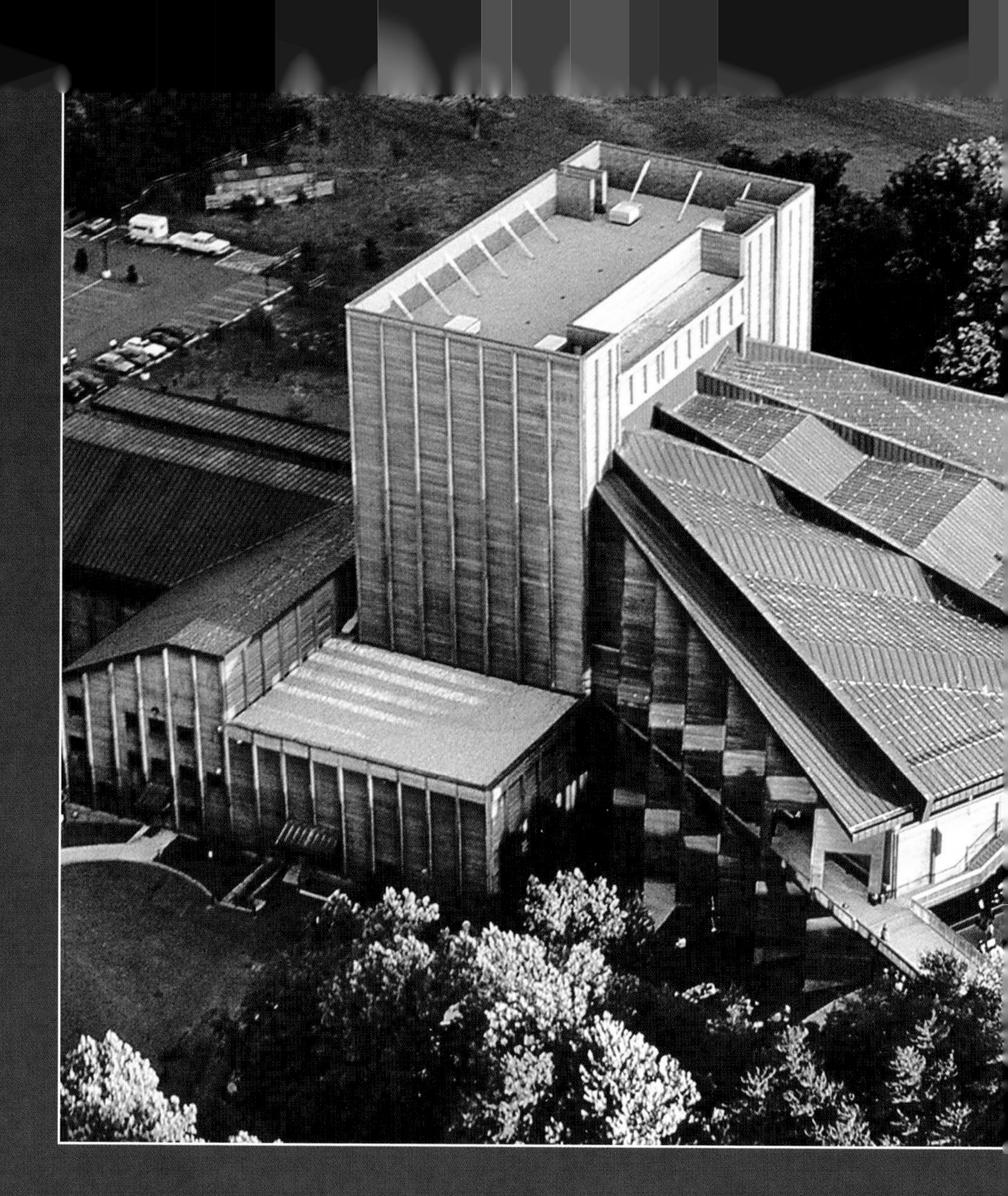

WOLF TRAP NATIONAL PARK FOR THE PERFORMING ARTS

Virginia

Wolf Trap is the only national park dedicated to the performing arts and stands as one of America's most respected and loved venues for live performances. The park is the product of a creative partnership between the National Park Service and a private, nonprofit organization, the Wolf Trap Foundation for the Performing Arts. Each organization delivers its special abilities to ensure that Wolf Trap remains a unique feature of the American cultural scene. Once a typical rural Virginia farm belonging to the park's benefactress, Catherine Filene Shouse, several original farm buildings, meadows, woodlands, and creeks surround the performance venues of the park, which make the experience of attending a performance truly special.

With a capacity of 7,000 patrons and boasting one of the nation's largest stages, the Filene Center is the centerpiece of Wolf Trap and a renowned performance amphitheater. The Filene Center's presentations suit a variety of interests with opera, dance, symphony, jazz, musical theater, and popular music performances. Nestled in a shady grove of trees near the Filene Center, the Children's Theatre-in-the-Woods presents family friendly dance, music, storytelling, puppetry, and musical theater.

The park is open daily. No entrance fee; ticket prices for performances vary. Performances are offered in the Filene Center from late May through mid-September. Children's Theatre-in-the-Woods performances run from late June through mid-August. Interpretive programs are offered year-round, and visitors may picnic at the park throughout the year.

www.nps.gov/wotr

PRINCE WILLIAM FOREST PARK

Virginia

Prince William Forest Park is an oasis of natural beauty and human history located only 35 miles south of Washington, D.C. The park protects the largest Piedmont forest in the national park system and a large portion of the beautiful Quantico Creek watershed. Thirty-seven miles of hiking trails and 21 miles of bicycle-accessible roads and trails traverse beneath a 15,000-acre canopy of leaves.

In the mid-1930s, this land was chosen to become parkland as part of a program aimed at building recreation facilities close to major cities. The Recreational Demonstration Area would provide relief for those who built the park and for those who used it. Two thousand men from the Civilian Conservation Corps earned a living in the park from 1934 to 1941, planting trees and building cabin camps in a rustic pioneer style. In these camps, children and single mothers would reap the benefits of recreating in the great outdoors—namely fitness and self-improvement.

During World War II, the park briefly closed to the general public as the Office of Strategic Services used the cabin camps to train intelligence operatives for life behind enemy lines. After the war, the park returned to the public and continues to serve the recreation needs of the American public.

www.nps.gov/prwi

CATOCTIN MOUNTAIN PARK

Maryland

Renew—to make new or fresh again. President Franklin Roosevelt sought ways to renew both land and people during the Depression era. In 1936, through the Works Progress Administration (WPA) and the Civilian Conservation Corps (CCC), land that could no longer support farming and traditional industries like charcoal and iron making was transformed into the Catoctin Recreational Demonstration Area. This action provided a new role for the land and new opportunities for workers. Today's visitors enjoy the benefits of their work and may also experience their own renewal of both body and spirit, experiencing the renewed forest habitat and scenic beauty of Catoctin Mountain Park.

Recreational opportunities abound, and visitors may enjoy camping in historic camps, hiking a trail, or discovering the almost lost art of charcoal making. They can explore the site of an old whiskey still, cross-country ski, fly-fish in Big Hunting Creek, or tent camp in Owens Creek Campground. Some find inspiration at several scenic overlooks; others search for wildlife or just take the opportunity to gather with family and friends.

As an outdoor classroom, Catoctin Mountain Park offers lifelong learning opportunities. Education programs meet local school curricula. Adults enjoy the challenge of nature identification with field guides in hand. Some shorter trails focus on cultural heritage and natural history with wayside signs explaining and describing features along the way.

From wildflowers to wildlife to autumn wow and winter wonder, Catoctin Mountain Park awaits visitors during all four seasons of the year.

www.nps.gov/cato

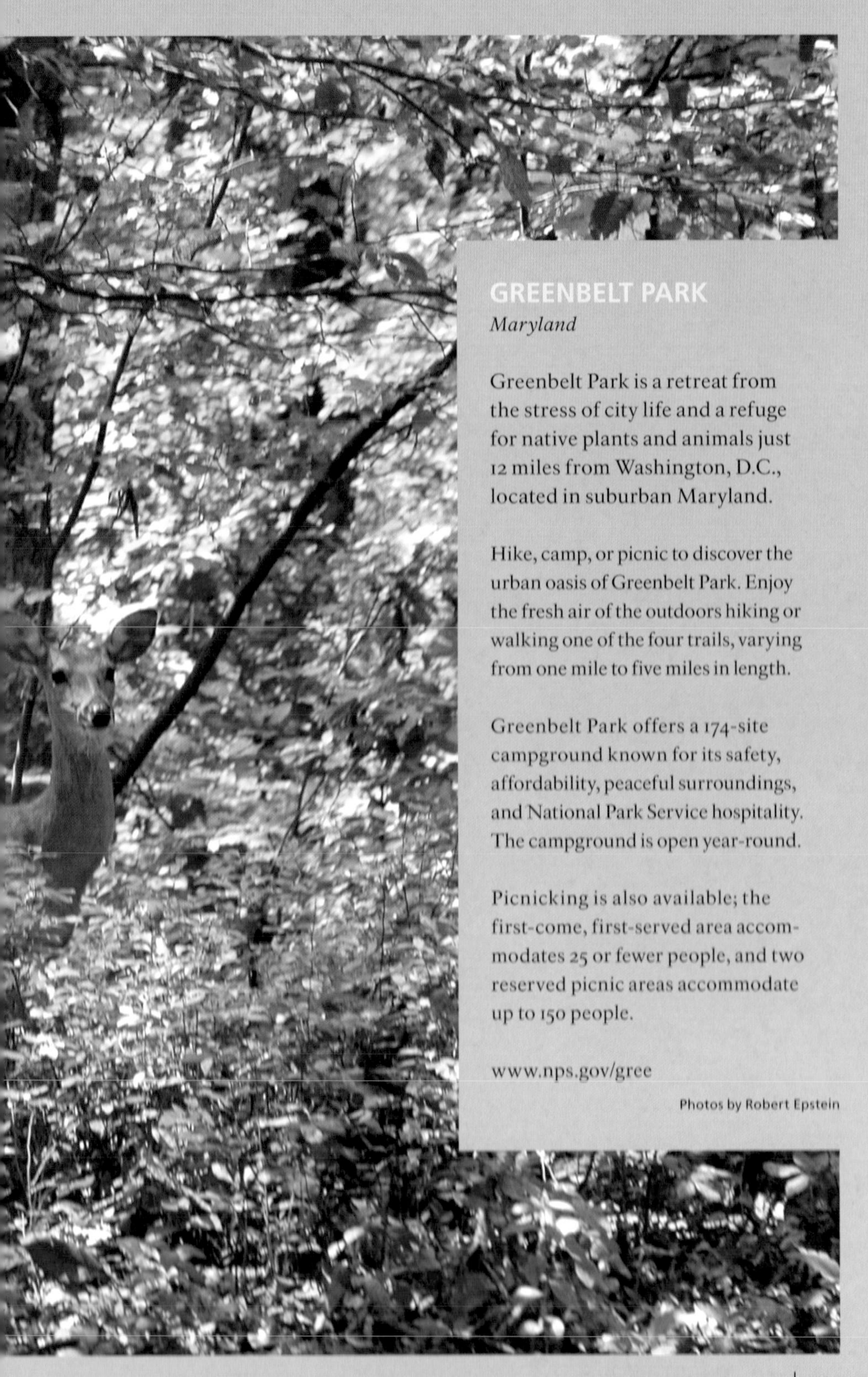

GREENBELT PARK

Maryland

Greenbelt Park is a retreat from the stress of city life and a refuge for native plants and animals just 12 miles from Washington, D.C., located in suburban Maryland.

Hike, camp, or picnic to discover the urban oasis of Greenbelt Park. Enjoy the fresh air of the outdoors hiking or walking one of the four trails, varying from one mile to five miles in length.

Greenbelt Park offers a 174-site campground known for its safety, affordability, peaceful surroundings, and National Park Service hospitality. The campground is open year-round.

Picnicking is also available; the first-come, first-served area accommodates 25 or fewer people, and two reserved picnic areas accommodate up to 150 people.

www.nps.gov/gree

Photos by Robert Epstein

OXON COVE PARK

Maryland

Located in the District of Columbia and Prince George's County, Maryland, Oxon Cove Park features the 63-acre Oxon Hill Farm, a working historic farm. Visitors can explore the early 19th-century farmhouse (Welby Manor), and historic barns, stables, and outbuildings. Animals, crops, orchards, and gardens are also found on the farm site. The park's 485 acres provide recreational opportunities for hiking, biking, and picnicking, and are an excellent resource for environmental studies, wildlife observation, and fishing.

Reservations are required for special programs, educational offerings, and popular activities such as milking cows, gathering eggs, and wagon rides.

www.nps.gov/oxhi

Photo by Robert Epstein

PISCATAWAY PARK

Maryland

Piscataway Park stretches for seven miles from Piscataway Creek to Marshall Hall on the Potomac River in southern Prince George's County, Maryland. This park was established in 1961 "to preserve for the benefit of present and future generations the historic and scenic values . . . of lands which provide the principal overview from the Mount Vernon Estate and Fort Washington."

For thousands of years, people have lived along the hospitable shore of the Potomac River where higher terraces meet coastal plains, and hillsides and ravines drain to marshland with a rich diversity of plant and animal life. Archeologists have found evidence of human presence here that dates back more than 9,000 years. In 1608, Captain John Smith visited the Moyaone village of the Piscataway Indians when he came by boat from Jamestown to explore and to establish new colonies. In 1979, the U.S. Congress authorized the burial of Chief Turkey Tayac, leader of the Piscataway Indian Nation Incorporated, on the shores of the park across from Mount Vernon.

With more than 4,600 acres of park and scenic easement lands, Piscataway Park is the largest remaining natural ecosystem in southern Maryland. Abundant wildlife, waterfowl, and countless species of plant life call this scenic natural area home. There are frequent sightings of bald eagles, beaver, and other wildlife that wander about in the delicate marsh areas of Accokeek Creek located in the heart of the park.

The circa 1725 Marshall Hall mansion, located on the southern end of the park, suggests the grace of plantation living and its eventual downfall. A 1981 fire destroyed all but the brick walls of the 18th-century tide-water mansion. The Marshall family thrived as planters on part of a land grant dating to 1662. With the end of the Civil War, slavery and the planters' way of life came to an end. Passing through a succession of owners, including an amusement park from 1895 until 1979, the final 446 acres of the Marshall Hall Amusement Park became part of the National Park Service in 1973.

Two of the original organizations that coordinated the founding of Piscataway Park in the late 1950s, the Alice Ferguson Foundation and the Accokeek Foundation, continue to provide environmental and cultural education

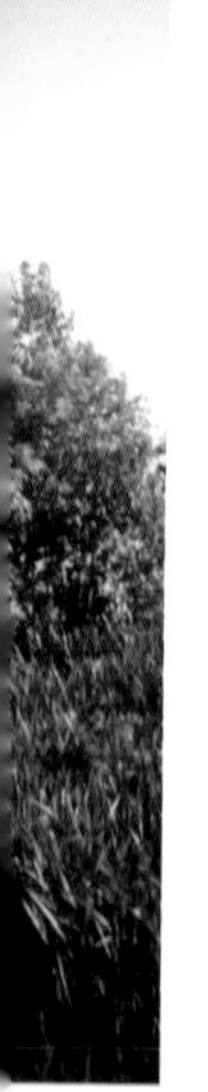

Photo by Robert Epstein

programs for the public in partnership with the National Park Service. At the National Colonial Farm, visitors can learn about 18th century farm life in early America when settlers struggled for a toehold on the continent. The Accokeek Foundation operates the farm as part of its mission to "preserve, protect and foster . . . the historic sites and relics, trees, plants and wildlife rapidly disappearing from an area of great natural beauty." The foundation also maintains an ecosystem farm and an arboretum displaying native trees of southern Maryland, including the rare American chestnut.

The Alice Ferguson Foundation operates the Hard Bargain Farm, an environmental education facility for grade school students from the metropolitan area. In addition, the foundation develops and coordinates numerous curriculum-based earth science, ecology, and conservation education and training programs for local teachers. This organization has worked in partnership with the National Park Service and many other organizations to implement programs for preserving resources and eliminating pollution while fostering stewardship among all ages.

Today, through continued partnerships with many like-minded organizations, Piscataway Park has become one of the most valued and highly protected natural and cultural resources in Maryland.

www.nps.gov/pisc
www.fergusonfoundation.org

Photo by Robert Epstein

POTOMAC HERITAGE NATIONAL SCENIC TRAIL

Maryland / Pennsylvania / Virginia / Washington, D.C.

A great life is one in which early dreams carry you through to old age. George Washington dreamed of a pathway for commerce between the Chesapeake Bay and the Forks of the Ohio River. Today you can travel sections of the Potomac Heritage National Scenic Trail to experience its changing geography—and share in Washington's dream.

An enterprise of many partners, the evolving Trail network traces the events and places at the heart of the nation's evolution and celebrates the rich heritage of the Potomac and upper Ohio river basins. One of 25 national scenic and historic trails in the National Trails System, the Potomac Heritage National Scenic Trail embraces a rich combination of natural areas, historic sites, and vibrant cities and towns while also providing superb outdoor recreation opportunities such as hiking, bicycling, boating, horseback riding, and cross-country skiing.

To date, the Trail network includes:

- The 184.5-mile historic towpath within the Chesapeake and Ohio National Historical Park;
- The 17-mile Mount Vernon Trail and 10-mile Potomac Heritage Trail within George Washington Memorial Parkway;
- Trails in Prince William Forest Park, Great Falls Park, and Piscataway Park;
- The Fort Circle Parks Trail, a greenbelt of parks connecting Abraham Lincoln's Civil War Defenses of Washington; and
- Numerous other trails and bicycling routes managed by local, regional, and state park agencies in Virginia, Maryland, and Pennsylvania; private organizations; and state departments of transportation.

The network, with its numerous opportunities to experience our nation's diverse natural and cultural heritage, continues to grow.

www.nps.gov/pohe

INDEX